WOOD CARVING
FOR BEGINNERS

by
CHARLES H. HAYWARD

WALL BRACKET : GOTHIC TRAY
BELLOWS : LINENFOLD PANEL
PARAKEET : BOOK ENDS
EGG & TONGUE MOULDING
PANEL WITH OAK AND LAUREL
LEAVES
CHIP CARVING : INCISED
LETTERING ETC.

WHAT THIS BOOK IS ABOUT . .

There is probably no occupation which links together art and craftsmanship in so ideal a fashion as wood carving. To imitate the natural fold of a leaf or catch the expression of a face calls for artistic appreciation : whilst the production of crisp, clean work calls for an understanding of grain, manual dexterity, and the other factors needed in the making of a good craftsman. One of the difficulties facing the man in the street is that of designs, and this we have endeavoured to overcome by giving them in full size wherever practicable. Thus a sheet of tracing paper and a piece of carbon paper are the only requirements. The tracing is taken direct from the design, and this transferred to the wood by means of the carbon paper. The designs could either be used in the particular way suggested, or they could be adapted to suit special items, or used in the decoration of furniture and other woodwork.

The opening chapter on tools and their sharpening should be read carefully, because sharp, well-conditioned tools are essential in carving. It is possible to make a blunt saw cut, or to take off a shaving with a plane which has lost its keenness : but good carving with blunt tools is impossible. And the curious thing is that, the softer the wood, the more razor-like the edge required to cut it cleanly.

As in other things, begin with a simple design before tackling more advanced work, and make a careful study of the examples of good carving to be seen in museums, churches, and so on. Note specially the way in which particular problems have been solved : how certain parts are undercut, how some edges are bevelled, and how a suggestion of delicacy is obtained without sacrifice of strength. Finally, keep on practising. Remember that, though you can learn much by studying, it is only in the practical work that you finally come to learn how to carve.

. . . CONTENTS . . .

WOOD CARVING FOR BEGINNERS

Tools and how to sharpen them

You cannot carve successfully unless you can sharpen your tools properly. Blunt tools merely cause the grain to crumble and leave a ragged, crude finish. A keen tool will cut across a piece of soft pine cleanly, leaving the crisp tool marks always associated with professional work.

CARVING tools are known by numbers as well as by size, and the system of this numbering can be somewhat confusing until you understand it. A common illusion is that all tools having the same number are made from the same sweep of circle. Actually this is not the case.

Numbering System.—The rule is that all tools of the same number have the same relative degree of curvature in proportion to their size. To take an obvious case, the shape of a No. 9 tool is a half-circle. Thus a ¼ in. No. 9 gouge is a semi-circle struck with ⅛ in. radius; similarly a 1 in. No. 9 gouge is a semi-circle struck with a ½ in. radius. This is made clear at A. The same principle applies to B in which the sweep is much flatter. Both curves represent a quarter circle, and both have the same number. This system is followed for all carving tools regardless of type.

Carving Chisel.—Let us now consider the various forms of carving tools. There is first the chisel, the edge of which is straight. It is the No. 1, and can be obtained with the edge ground straight across or at an angle, in which case it is known as a corner chisel (see Fig. 1). Its sharpening differs from that of ordinary woodworking chisels in that both sides are bevelled. In the illustration the bevel appears flat for clearness, but in actual practice, although flat for the greater part, it is rounded over into the main blade so that there is no definite line where the bevel begins. This, incidentally, applies to all carving tools.

Straight and Curved Gouges.—The straight gouge, so named because its shaft is straight, is the most widely used tool, and it is available in a wide range of sizes and numbers. It is the maid-of-all-work tool to the carver. The curved gouge is needed for work for which the straight gouge would be unsuitable. For instance, in hollowing out a fairly deep depression such as in a wooden bowl it is essential. The straight gouge would merely dig in.

Bent Chisels and Gouges.—For recessing the background of a design the bent chisel is imperative. It will reach into corners which could

not be negotiated by a straight chisel. There are three forms: that in which the edge is at right angles, and the right and left corner bent chisels (see illustration). The use of these soon becomes clear to the worker. They will reach into sharp corners more acute than a right angle.

The front bent gouge comes in for jobs similar to those for which the curved gouge is needed, but it is wanted for sharper curves. For instance, for cutting in the hollow shapes of Gothic trefoils, etc., the front bent gouge is needed. The back-bent gouge has limited use, but is required sometimes for hollow-shaped edgings which are rounded in section, and for other tricky parts.

V Tools.—Parting or V tools are used mostly in the preliminary setting in of the work, and also for certain veining operations. Three angles are

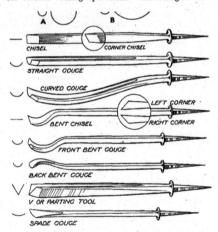

FIG. I. THE VARIOUS TYPES OF CARVING TOOLS
For the ordinary run of work the straight gouge should always be used. In fact, except for special jobs, the beginner need not bother about the curved and bent gouges at all.

1

USE A FINE QUALITY OILSTONE FOR YOUR TOOLS

FIG. 2. STAGES IN SHARPENING GOUGE WITH OILSTONE AND SLIP
To the left the outside bevel is being rubbed down. A is a section showing the inside bevel. B. Forming the inside bevel with the oilstone slip. C. How outer corners are taken off to reduce the thickness.

available, these being approximately 45, 65, and 90 degrees. All can be obtained either straight (as shown) or in curved or front bent form.

Spade Tools.—Spade gouges are usually kept for the fine finishing operations. The edge, being wider than the main shaft, can reach beneath projections and into corners. It is a delicate tool and is unsuitable for heavy chopping work. A variety of it is the long-pod gouge in which the difference between the width of the edge and the shaft is not so marked.

The only other tool to be noted, though it has limited use, is the macaroni tool, which is used sometimes for finishing around designs in which the background is recessed. It is rather like a flat, angular U in section.

SHARPENING THE TOOLS

Differing from ordinary wood-working tools, carving tools are sharpened on both sides. In fact, there is almost as much bevel on the inside of a gouge as the outside. Consequently it takes a long time to put new tools into really good condition. The outside bevel already exists, but it takes many sharpenings with the oilstone slip to produce the bevel inside. With new tools, then, once a satisfactory outside bevel has been attained, any subsequent sharpening should be done inside with the slip until eventually a good bevel has been produced here. Still, even with a new tool you can do perfectly good work if the quality of the edge is right.

The Gouge.—Let us take an ordinary gouge : the size is immaterial as the principle is the same for all. Rub it on the oilstone as shown in Fig. 2 with a rocking movement so that every part of the bevel is rubbed. The stone should be fine, but a coarse one can be used at first, providing the tool is finished on a fine grade. The angle is low—about 15 degrees. When a burr has been turned up a stone slip of the same curvature as the gouge or a little less is rubbed inside as at B, Fig. 2. Be careful to keep the edge square with the sides and rub the tool equally along its entire edge.

A shows the extent of the bevel that is ultimately formed. This shows the bevels clearly defined for clearness, but in actual practice they should curve into the body of the tool gradually. It is a good plan to take off the corners of the gouge as at C, as it reduces a thickness which is often in the way when working in sharp angles and corners.

When a tool has become gashed or its edge is out of shape it should be stood vertically on the stone and be rubbed until it is square, or the gash has been removed. The flat so formed gives a definite line up to which to work when sharpening afresh. In bad cases the gouge must be re-ground.

Stropping.—To produce the superfine edge essential for good work stropping is necessary. Obtain a piece of leather about 8 ins. by 3 ins., oil it to make it soft and pliable, and dress it with a mixture of oil and the finest emery powder. It should be kept under cover because any large grit which may fall upon it will soon ruin the edges of tools.

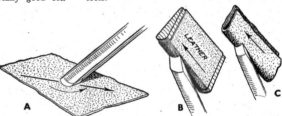

FIG. 3.
METHOD OF STROPPING. STROP IS DRESSED WITH OIL AND FINE EMERY
A shows the outer bevel being stropped. The strop lies flat on the bench. B. Use of special strop for inside bevel. C. Strop folded for use on inside bevel.

DRESS YOUR STROP WITH FINE EMERY AND OIL

A, Fig. 3, shows the first process, that of rubbing the bevelled side. Maintain the same angle and revolve the tool as it is drawn diagonally backwards so that every part of the edge is reached. Never dub over the tool in order to reach the edge quickly. It is false economy in the long run because the strop will soon fail to produce an edge, and rubbing down on the stone becomes necessary. Actually a carving tool will go for weeks or months with no other attention than that of stropping providing it is properly used.

The inside of the tool is stropped also, and a piece of leather glued round a suitably shaped block is excellent (see B). The curvature of the block should be rather less than that of the tool. Another plan which is particularly useful for smaller tools is to fold up the strop as at C, or even to use just the edge to fit into very small tools.

V Tools.—These in a way may be regarded as two chisels joined together at an angle, except that the inside surfaces have to be sharpened as in the case of the gouge. Fig. 4 shows how each bevel is rubbed down in turn, and the inside then dealt with as at D. There is one important point to watch, however. If the bevels are just rubbed flat on the stone and nothing more, a curious point will be found at the corner as at A. This is because the inside of the V tool, although theoretically a sharp corner, is in reality slightly rounded (see B at x). To get rid of this point the corner of the tool must be rubbed lightly with a rocking movement as at C. It will be realised that one reason why the inside corner is slightly rounded is that the oilstone slip (see D) used for the inside bevel is bound to lose its sharp corner, and this causes a round rather than a sharp angle.

Chisels.—These are sharpened on the oilstone similarly to an ordinary woodworking chisel, except that the bevel is considerably lower and that both sides are bevelled.

Bent Tools.—Keep the lower bevel flat on the stone, and give a slight bevel on top. Otherwise the sharpening and stropping is the same as in other gouges and chisels.

Bench.—Have a good, sturdy table or bench about 3 ft. or 3 ft. 3 ins. high and stand up to your

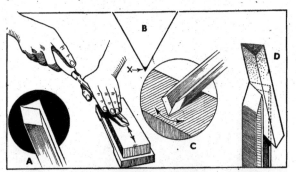

FIG. 4. SHARPENING V TOOL ON OILSTONE, AND USING SLIP
A. How point is formed at corner of V tool.   B. Reason why the point occurs.   It is owing to the inner thickness at X.   C. Rubbing corner of tool to remove the point. D. Using slip to give inside bevel.

work. Place it so that you either face the light or have the light to your left. Carving in the open with light all round is not so good because you cannot see the shadows formed by the tool marks.

Cramps.—To hold the work steady a couple of thumb screws or G cramps are needed. The carver's cramp is ideal for some work as it leaves the entire surface free from obstructions. The pointed screw at the end is forced into the underside of the work, the stem passed through a hole in the bench, and the curved nut tightened beneath. It is unsuitable for thin wood as there is insufficient thickness for the screw to bite.

PRELIMINARY KIT	
Straight Gouges :	
No. 7, $\frac{1}{2}$ in.	No. 8, $\frac{1}{4}$ in.
No. 4, $\frac{1}{2}$ in.	No. 5, $\frac{1}{4}$ in.
No. 3, $\frac{3}{8}$ in.	No. 4, $\frac{1}{4}$ in.
Bent chisels :	
No. 25, $\frac{1}{4}$ in.	V tool, $\frac{1}{4}$ in.
No. 25, $\frac{1}{16}$ in.	

USEFUL ADDITIONS

Straight Gouges—No. 4, $\frac{1}{4}$ in., No. 5, $\frac{1}{8}$ in.
U Gouge—No. 11, $\frac{3}{16}$ in., No. 11, $\frac{1}{8}$ in.
Corner Chisel—No. 2, $\frac{1}{16}$ in.
Bent Chisel—No. 24, $\frac{1}{8}$ in.
Bent Chisel—Right corner, No. 22, $\frac{1}{8}$ in.
Left corner, No. 23, $\frac{1}{8}$ in.

Fine oilstone and slips to fit the gouges. Strops can be made from leather dressed with the finest emery powder and oil.

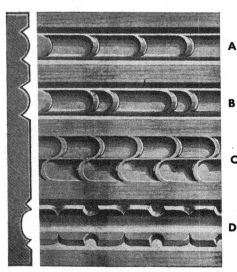

FIG. I. EXAMPLES OF SIMPLE GOUGE CUT DECORATION
A, B, and C are of a similar character, consisting of a slightly sloping upright cut with the waste gouged away horizontally. At D the cuts are made at the edges of a hollow. They slope into V channels at each side.

SIMPLE
GOUGE   CUTS

These simple cuts are based on the shape of the tool and, apart from teaching control of the gouge, form a most effective decoration. They are not difficult to cut, but neatness and accuracy are essential.

THERE are certain elementary forms of carving that are suggested by the shape of the gouges. Back in the oak period of furniture men realised the value of simple gouge cuts and used them with considerable effect. They form an excellent start for the beginner because the work gives an initiation into the handling of the tools, and at the same time they can be used with good effect in any piece of furniture he may be making. A few examples are given in Figs. 1 and 2, and it will be recognised how effective they can be. There are, of course, almost endless variations which can be worked out ; the reader will find it most interesting as well as good practice to experiment in finding new forms of cuts.

Taking the example A, Fig. 1, this can be carved on a flat surface if preferred, though the effect is enhanced if a flat bead is cut first. This bead can be worked with the scratch or it can be cut entirely with carving tools. The former method is advisable. for a start because it is simpler. Having worked this the cuts should be spaced out with a pair of dividers so that they fill in the length conveniently. Only the position of the upright cuts need be marked.

Downward Cuts.—Using a gouge of about the size and shape shown at *a*, Fig. 3 ($\frac{1}{4}$ in., No. 8) make a cut at a slight angle sloping towards the waste as shown in Fig. 4. Do not hold the gouge upright because this tends

to leave a rather weak edge. In any case the slope has a better effect because the light catches the surface. In softwood pressure with the hands is sufficient, but in oak a mallet can be used. The second cut starts near the next notch and slopes into the first cut. In its simplest form (B, Fig. 4) the cut runs straight down. A richer effect is obtained, however, by bringing it to its full width almost at once, continuing with its sides parallel as at A. It will usually be found more convenient to make all the downward cuts first, and then scoop out all the notches. If they are finished individually they should be cut from right to left in the example at A (Fig. 2). Otherwise the wood may tend to crumble when the subsequent downward cuts are made.

A point to remember (and this applies to all carving) is that the waste wood must actually be cut away by the tool. It is useless to try to scrape away chips and hairs of wood. The cuts must meet so that the chips come away cleanly of their own accord. This means that, since the edge of the gouge runs straight across at right angles with its length, it will cut slightly beneath the centre portion of the downward cut when the horizontal cut is being made. For this reason it is advisable to reach down to the finished depth as soon as possible to avoid making unnecessary marks.

Control of Gouge.—Fig. 5 shows the gouge in use. In practice the left-hand should grasp the blade more securely. The right hand provides the forward movement, whilst the left hand guides the tool and exerts a certain amount of back pressure to prevent it from overrunning. In fact, the movement is largely the result of forward pressure by the right hand and backward pressure by the left. Only in this way is the tool kept from bursting forward in the event of the wood fibres giving suddenly. The work, of course, is held down by a cramp or handscrew.

B and C in Fig. 1 are variations of the same idea. D, however, is rather different. It requires the use of more tools. In this case two V cuts are made and between them a hollow as shown in the section. Four marking-out lines are needed, these representing the sides of the V cuts. They can be drawn in with the rule and finger.

Using the V Tool.—The V tool (*c*, Fig. 3) is tricky to use because it is liable to follow the grain of the wood. It takes considerable practice to bring it under control. Do not try to take it down to its full depth straightway. Start midway between the pencil lines and work gradually along in short cuts, grasping the blade tightly in the left hand. Gradually deepen the cut until the sides reach to the pencil lines. The hollow centre is best formed by making a cut at each side with a fairly quick gouge (*a*) and removing the centre with a flatter one (*b*), so that the section is more or less elliptical (see section in Fig. 1).

To produce the carved effect space out the notches, using either dividers or cutting a stencil. Cut the rounded portions first, using the gouge (*b*, Fig. 3). It should slope at a slight angle as in the previous examples, and should lean over so that the edge of the blade cuts square against the outer side of the V groove as in Fig. 1. The waste is removed with the skew chisel (*d*, Fig. 3), the bevel of this lying flat against the groove.

In Fig. 2 the diagonal cuts at the bottom are cut across a flat,

FIG. 2. MORE EFFECTIVE PATTERNS EASILY FORMED WITH THE GOUGE
It is unnecessary to draw in every curve, but the position of the corresponding details should be stepped out with dividers or marked by means of a stencil.

rounded section, and thus give a spiral effect. It will be found that one side of the hollow is smooth whilst the other is liable to tear out. This necessitates taking the gouge in both directions. As the tool is taken into the side it can be given a twisting movement, one corner curling away and free from the wood whilst the other cuts the angle. Cut in at the ends with the skew chisel (*d*, Fig. 3).

FIG. 3. FULL-SIZE TOOL SHAPES

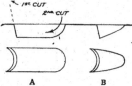

A   B

FIG. 4. HOW 1st CUTS SLOPE SLIGHTLY

FIG. 5. FORMING THE HOLLOWS AFTER THE UPRIGHT CUTS ARE MADE
The forward movement is provided by the right hand. The left hand guides the tool and exerts a certain amount of backward pressure to avoid over-running. Actually the fingers should curl more round the blade to grip it more securely. This is not shown here as it would conceal the blade and the work too much.

CHISEL CUTS

FIG. 1. FIVE PATTERNS CUT WITH THE CHISEL
This form of decoration is most effective when used around the edge of a table or cabinet top. It is of a quite different character from that of a cheap applied embossed moulding. The chisel is used throughout.

SHARP tools are vital to work of this kind. Keep the strop handy, using it little and often.

Design A.—To simplify the cutting it is desirable to arrange the depression widths to suit the chisel to be used. Thus, if a ¼-in. chisel is chosen the depressions should be a trifle over a ¼ in. To mark out, measure the depressions and the distance between them on a piece of card, and use this to mark out along the edge as at A, Fig. 2.

Note that the depressions do not reach either to the edge or to the corner of the rebate, but start about 1/16 in. in or a little less. To mark this, draw in two lines in pencil parallel with the edge as shown at A, Fig. 2.

The first cuts are made with a wide chisel across the grain at each side of the depressions, the chisel bevel facing the depression in every case. Hold the chisel at an angle as at B, Fig. 2, so that the cutting edge cuts in deeply where required without penetrating near the outer corner. Go along the length of the work in this way. Next take the ¼ in. chisel and cut down *with* the grain at the end of the depression, sloping the chisel at the same angle as when cutting the sides. The grain is thus cut all round, enabling the waste to be cleanly pared away as at C.

Design B.—The groove is first worked, the width being slightly greater than that of the chisel to be used. Step out the length of the steps with dividers, and square a line across at each. Cut down across the grain with chisel and mallet, the bevel facing the low part of the step (A, Fig. 3). The chisel should lean slightly away from the step. Now cut down at each side, the chisel lining up with the sides of the groove. Here again the chisel must be held at an angle so that the cutting edge penetrates deeply only where required. This is shown at A, Fig. 3. Finish off as at B.

Design C.—This is rather more difficult to cut cleanly. Mark out as at A, Fig. 4, noting that the sides of the squares do not quite meet either at the centre or at top and bottom. To ensure this draw two lines close together spaced equally at each side of the centre and work from there. Draw in the sides of the squares with mitre square.

Cut down the sides of the squares, holding the chisel at an angle as at B, Fig. 4, so that the cut is deep at one end and runs out at the other. Finish off as at C, taking care not to let the chisel cut into the pencil lines near the edge.

Design D.—This is done in two separate stages. Mark out as at A, Fig. 5, giving main sloping lines only. Cut down as in the previous examples and ease away the waste to form sloping depressions (see B). Finish the whole work up to this stage, then mark out in the depressions the lines of the inner shapes as at C. It is then only a matter of cutting down the smaller depressions and paring away the waste as at D.

Design E.—Mark out as at A, Fig. 6, squaring across the edge the positions of the various members and putting in also on the adjoining surface a line marking the depth of the sloping surfaces. Cut down with chisel and mallet the lines marking the deepest part of the slopes as at B. If, however, the small members are very short there is a danger that the wood may crumble away at the point X. To obviate this cut in lightly only and ease away the wood at the side as at C. The cut can then be taken down to the full depth. Afterwards the correct slope can be eased away *with* the grain. It will pay to cut either all the large surfaces first, then the smaller ones, or vice versa. It will be necessary to cut down with the chisel in line with the rebate to ensure a clean finish.

6

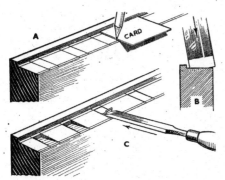

FIG. 2. MARKING AND CUTTING PATTERN (A).
A. Shows use of square card for marking.
B. Downward cuts with chisel.   C. Paring waste.

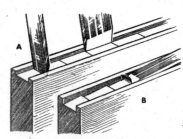

FIG. 3. HOW PATTERN (B) IS CUT.
After chopping down with chisel as at A, the sloping faces
are eased away as at B.

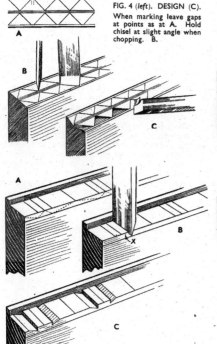

FIG. 4 (left). DESIGN (C).
When marking leave gaps
at points as at A. Hold
chisel at slight angle when
chopping. B.

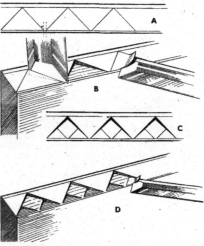

FIG. 5. DETAILS OF CUTTING DESIGN (D).
After marking, A, cut main triangle, B. Draw smaller triangles,
C, and cut out as at D.

FIG. 6 (left). METHOD OF MARKING AND CUTTING (E)
Marking is shown at A, chopping down at B, and preliminary
paring at C.

7

CARVED BOOKSTAND

The woodwork of this is simple. The base is lap-dovetailed to the ends as in Fig. 3, and feet are screwed on beneath.

FIG. I. ATTRACTIVE BOOKSTAND WITH CARVED ENDS IN OAK
This makes a useful item and it provides a most interesting piece of carving. Few tools are needed. Oak is the most suitable wood.

ONE half of the design is shown full size in Fig. 2. Transfer to the wood with carbon or tracing paper. Put in the circles with compasses.

Cut out two pieces of ¼ in. stuff slightly full in length, and plane them to the finished width. Prepare the base also and cut the joints. Do not assemble, however. Draw in a centre upright line on each end and place the paper with the half design upon the wood so that the two centre lines coincide. Press a couple of drawing pins into waste parts of the wood to hold it, and, slipping a sheet of carbon paper beneath, go over the complete design. Reverse the paper on to the other half of the wood (the indentation will show through), and draw in this. The outline can be sawn out and finished off with file and glasspaper.

Outlining the Design.—Now for the carving. The first step is to sink the groundwork so that the straps are left in projection. Go round the design first with a quick gouge a short way from the line on the waste side. This eases the work of chopping downwards since the wood crumbles away. This is especially the case when hard oak is being carved. The depth should be slightly less than the finished size.

You will have to select a gouge which approximates to the curve when chopping down. In the case of concave shapes (the inner sides of the circles, for instance) the gouge, if anything, should be slightly more acute than the circle, otherwise the corners are liable to dig in. The reverse applies for convex shapes, the gouge being rather flatter. Notice from Fig. 6 that the gouge is held at a slight angle rather than upright. Generally it is advisable to cut the cross grain first. In the present case the depth is about ⅛ in., and the tool can be taken down to this straightway. Let the gouge lightly overlap the last cut so that every part of the shape is cut.

Sinking the Groundwork.—Now follows the sinking of the groundwork. Choose a fairly acute gouge of about ¼ in. size and cut away the waste as shown in Fig. 4. Generally it is easier to work across the grain rather than with it, though it is not always practicable. The aim in this work is to recess all parts to the same depth. This is really important if a satisfactory result is to be obtained. After a little practice you will be able to judge with your eye, but in the meantime a matchstick passed through a hole in a little piece of card makes a simple yet effective depth gauge. This acute tool will leave the work with a series of well-pronounced ridges upon it, and these are taken out with a flatter gouge. You will not get rid of the marks altogether —indeed, it is not desirable to do so because the facets give an interesting play of light.

For the acute corners you will need a bent chisel, but use the ordinary flat gouge as far as possible. In the portion beneath the main design, the acute gouge only is used, and the direction of the cuts should follow an ordered plan as in Fig. 2, as they have a decorative effect when done in this way. Do not make them perfectly flat, but dig in the gouge slightly at the beginning of the cut and straighten out as the circles are reached.

Straps.—Cut downwards across the straps where necessary and slope away the wood at each side to the extent of about ¹⁄₁₆ in. as at B (Fig. 6). Avoid an abrupt slope such as that at A. When satisfactory the straps are made slightly hollow.

A good plan is to make a preliminary cut in the centre of the strap all round, and then work first one side of the strap and then the other, altering the direction of the cut to suit the grain.

8

THE DESIGN IN FULL SIZE AND METHODS OF WORKING

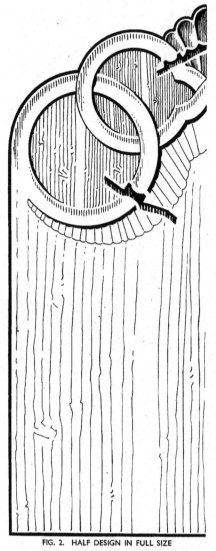

FIG. 2. HALF DESIGN IN FULL SIZE

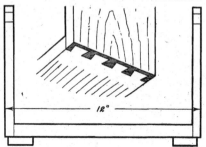

FIG. 3. SIZE AND CONSTRUCTION OF BOOKSTAND

FIG. 4. USING GOUGE TO SINK THE GROUNDWORK

FIG. 5. HOW STRAPS ARE HOLLOWED

FIG. 6. AVOID ABRUPT SLOPES (A) WHEN INTERLACING. MAKE THEM GRADUAL AS AT B.

9

GOTHIC
WALL BRACKET

This design is based upon the leaf work found frequently during the Decorated period of Gothic architecture. The work could be simplified considerably by omitting the raised veins. They not only necessitate the cutting away of a great deal of wood at each side, but they reduce the area in which the tool has to work, and small details are always more difficult to deal with. At the same time they add greatly to the effect and are really worth the labour involved.

Sinking the Background.—You will realise that the leaves stand up from a recessed background which extends to the narrow border. This has first to be roughly sunk so as to free the leaves from the surrounding wood. Its finished depth is ¼ in., but it should be stopped short of this because when the outlines of the leaves are cut in finally there are bound to be tool marks, and these could not be removed if the ground were down to the finished depth.

Figs. 3 and 4 show the stages in the work. A fairly large V tool, say, No. 39, ⁵⁄₁₆ in., is used to cut around the leaves, as in Fig. 3. Note that no attempt is made to follow the shape of the small lobes. The tool is taken straight around the main outline which is approximately a series of squares. It is an advantage if the tool is held at an angle so that the cut against the leaf is more upright than the other (see A, Fig. 4). In the case of the main border this is best cut in with a veiner (³⁄₁₆ in., No. 11). Where the berries occur at the top leave triangular pieces from which they can be carved later.

The bulk of the waste can be removed with a large, fairly quick gouge, say No. 7 ½ in. Make long, even cuts either straight across the grain or diagonally. It is easier than cutting with the grain and not so liable to splinter out. Fig. 3 shows this stage. With a flatter gouge, No. 4, ½ in., you can make the groundwork approximately flat around the design, and can take it to within ¹⁄₃₂ in. to ¹⁄₁₆ in. of the finished depth, but do not attempt to finish it at this stage. The small spaces between the leaves will require the use of smaller tools, and also the grounding tools ¼ in., No. 25, and ⅛ in., 23 skew tool.

Modelling.—A study of the undulations of the leaves will reveal that in the main they take the form of concentric circles (Figs. 1 and 2). These have now to be cut, but first note that some of the leaves overlap the others. With the V tool run round the main outline of the top leaves, cutting in not more than ⅛ in. Then gradually slope away the wood of the lower leaves so that they appear to pass beneath.

With a pair of compasses mark out on each leaf the circles shown by the dotted lines in Fig. 2. Take the No. 8, ¼ in. gouge and cut out the hollows around the circles, changing the direction of the cut if the grain tends to tear out. Where a leaf is lowered to pass beneath an adjoining one the hollow is cut correspondingly deep.

FIG. I. BRACKET FOR LAMP OR CLOCK
The bracket measures 12 ins. by 6 ins. and has a semi-circular shelf 2¾ ins. deep. Oak ½ in. thick is used throughout, except for the shelf, which is of ⅞ in. stuff.

THE construction of this bracket is fairly obvious. Both shelf and bracket are held to the back with screws, and the bracket is either slot-screwed to the shelf or is let into a groove. In plan the shelf is semi-circular and has a hollow moulding worked around its top edge. This, incidentally, makes a quite interesting job to do with a carving gouge. A chamfer is first worked down to pencil lines, and the hollow then cut in.

So far as the back panel is concerned, prepare a full-size drawing of this, tracing from the design in Fig. 2. The shapes at the top are drawn in with compasses; also the main sweep at the bottom. Transfer it to the wood (½ in. oak) by means of carbon paper. Saw out the outline and clean it up.

10

Now follows the shaping of the individual lobes of the leaves as in Fig. 6. First cut in the deep channels, using a small quick gouge at the inner ends and flatter ones along the sides. You will have to select gouges in accordance with the curve. Having cut in vertically remove the waste with the $\frac{1}{16}$ in. grounding tool, No. 25. When forming the small lobes you can with advantage slightly undercut. This makes the leaves stand out better. Take the cuts well in and then finish off the groundwork, finishing off with a No. 3 flat gouge, $\frac{1}{4}$ in. or $\frac{3}{8}$ in. wide. You will not remove all the gouge marks, but this is neither necessary nor desirable.

Fig. 7 shows the next stage in which the corners of the hollowed-out circles are rounded off. This should be done in long crisp cuts. Avoid a multitude of little niggling chips and strive for a broad

FIG. 2. THE CARVING IN FULL SIZE. IN SMALLER DIAGRAM SQUARES EQUAL 1 ″

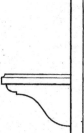

effect rather than a dead smooth finish. Some of the little lobes turn down to the background whilst others bend upwards, and with a few deft cuts you can give this effect. Don't attempt to make all the leaves alike—a little variety is an advantage. Another point is that you can use discretion when carving the overlapping leaves. Owing to your being unable to cut them in deeply it is as well to make the lobes here bend upwards.

Veining.—For cutting the veins you need a small veiner—No. 11, $\frac{1}{16}$ in. Of course, the work you have done so far will have removed your original marks, and you will have to put them in afresh

11

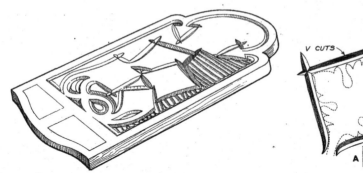

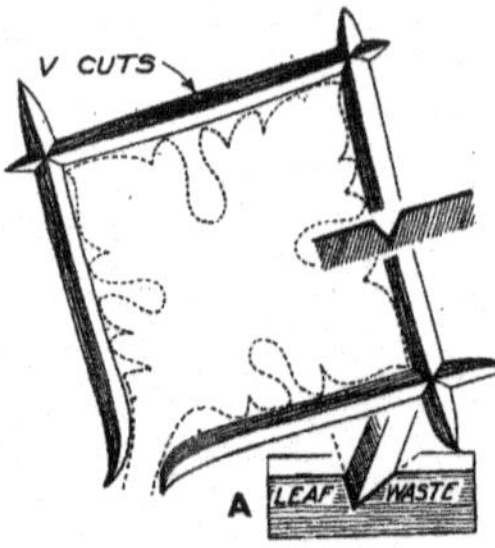

FIG. 3. HOW DESIGN IS OUTLINED WITH V TOOL AND BACKGROUND CUT AWAY   FIG. 4. V-TOOL OUTLINING

with the pencil. A single line marking the centre of each vein is all you need. At each side make an incision with the veiner, leaving a little square between. As the ends of the leaf are reached the cuts should converge so that the veins die away to nothing ; they should become shallower for the same reason. Of course, you will repeatedly have to change the direction of the cut owing to the undulations of the leaf. These cuts leave the vein between practically square in section, and the top corners can now be rounded over. At each side the wood will have to be eased away, and whilst this is being done any finishing touches to the modelling can be given. For instance, some of the lobes are hollow in section, and a small hollow is carried around the eyes ; that is, the four deep cuts which separate the main lobes.

When all is satisfactory, run around the edges of the whole design with a small flat gouge so as to form the chamfer (see Fig. 8). Here is a hint to make clean inner corners between the lobes. Put a flat gouge in the corner so that it halves the angle,

and make a slight cut with it. The latter should lean over so that its edge is at about the same angle as the chamfer. When the latter is worked the waste chip comes away cleanly since the gouge works right into the corner cut already made. Before passing the work finally look at it from all angles and observe whether the curves are sweet and continuous. It may easily happen that a shape which is fair when looked at from the front may appear bent and distorted when viewed from the side. It is due to the undulating surface.

Finally the stalks can be worked. The outline being cut round, the interlaced effect should be given by sloping back those parts which appear to pass beneath others. The section is rounded by taking off the two corners at 45 degrees and then removing the four flat corners that this produces. This gives a series of small facets, and by undercutting the sides a good effect of roundness is produced. Finally, with the small veiner No. 11, $\frac{1}{16}$ in., give the twisted effect. Work from the centre outwards and downwards.

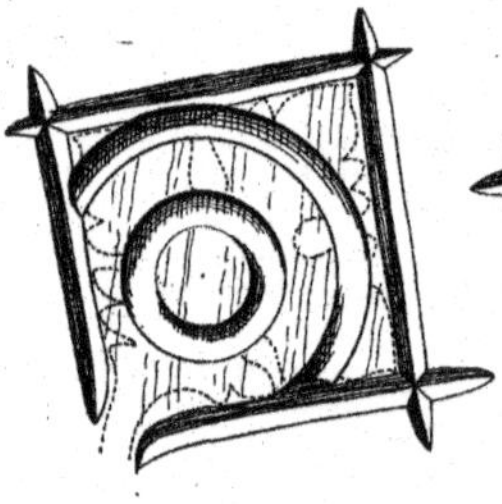

FIG. 5.
CUTTING CIRCULAR
HOLLOWS

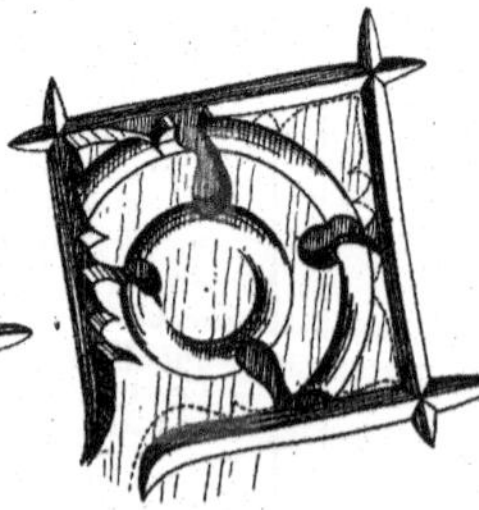

FIG. 6.
OUTLINE CUT IN

FIG. 7.
SMOOTHING EDGES
OF HOLLOWS

FIG. 8. VEINS CUT

PARAKEET

This is a wonderfully interesting piece of work to carve, and it makes a delightful ornament. Finished in bright natural colours, it is at once a striking piece for the staircase window, mantelshelf, or corner bracket. If preferred it could be adapted to form one of a pair of book ends. The whole thing can be completed with no more than six or seven carving tools.

PREPARE a piece of wood to finish 11¼ ins. by 3⅜ ins. square. This allows an extra 1½ ins. in the length at the bottom and enables the work to be gripped with the cramp and be handled freely. Actually the size can be varied if wood of the exact size is not available. A mellow and fairly soft hardwood is ideal to use, though a piece of an old deal staircase newel from a blitzed house was used for the bird shown here.

Marking Out.—It is useless to draw out the whole thing in detail on the wood because the marks would be almost wholly removed as chips were taken off.

Make a tracing of the main outline in Fig. 2 as seen from the front elevation, and draw this out on front and back of the wood. As the head is turned, the two sides will not balance exactly at the top. This main outline will enable you to see just what preliminary wood can be removed. This is

shown in Fig. 3. Make saw cuts across the grain and chisel away the waste.

Preliminary Shaping.—We now have the bird very approximately shaped as seen from the front. A similar shaping is now required from the side. Fig. 2 shows the parts (shown shaded) that can be sawn and chiselled away, and the work at this stage of completion is given in Fig. 4. Take care not to saw in too deeply.

Account has now to be taken of the fact that the head is turned, because, whereas the body balances when viewed exactly from the front, the head must balance when viewed from the direction in which it is looking. To do this draw in a line across the top as shown in Fig. 4 (the angle can be seen from the plan view to the left).

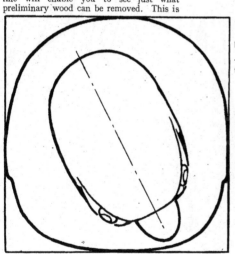

FULL SIZE PLAN SHOWING ANGLE OF HEAD

13

FIG. 2. FRONT AND SIDE VIEWS IN FULL SIZE. PLAN IS SHOWN ON PREVIOUS PAGE

14

REMEMBER THAT THE CARVING IS SEEN FROM ALL ANGLES

Bosting In.—It is as well at the outset to give the head a definite direction as otherwise the form of the thing may be lost. If this is your first experience at work of this kind you will probably have to feel your way to a considerable extent, but you know the width of the head, and if you measure each side of the centre line you cannot go wrong. Fig. 5 shows the corners cut away to form roughly the head. For the beak just allow a rectangular chunk. Detail follows later. Use a large flat gouge for this work.

The body of the bird is rounded in section, and you can now take over the corners as in Fig. 5. Start with what is more or less a flat chamfer, and afterwards round off the corners. Do the whole thing in stages—that is, all the chamfering and then all the rounding. It helps to keep the whole balanced. A flat chisel is the simplest tool to use for this work where heavy chips have to be removed.

Try also to make the direction of the cuts help in the general form of the bird. For instance, consider the direction of the feathers and try to make the cuts follow them. This is especially important in the final stages of the work. It may not always prove practicable, but try to follow the plan.

Using the No. 7 ½ in. gouge, cut in the general form of the neck. This will enable you to form the shoulders and make the head more shapely. Note that the latter is rather flat at the top and slopes downwards towards the rear. Chip away first one side, then the other, so that it is balanced, and get into the habit of looking at the work from *all* angles.

Beak.—You can now shape this. Form the profile first, then mark a centre line around it as a guide to keeping the two sides alike. Waste away the sides, and where they join the face use the small U gouge No. 11. When approximately right make horizontal cuts with a quick gouge to form the mouth, and ease away the waste of the lower beak. A sloping cut running upwards into the horizontal one forms the actual mouth.

Eyes.—It will be seen from Figs. 1 and 2 that a hollow is cut both above and below the eye, and that the intervening wood is rounded, so forming cheeks. The rounded gouges, Nos. 8 (¼ in.) and 5 (¼ in.) are used for the hollow cuts and the flatter gouges for the rounding. Mark in the eyes, about ⅜ in. diam., and, using the No. 8 (¼ in.) gouge, stab downwards into the wood, shifting the position of the tool to form the complete circle. Ease away the wood outside, using the small flat gouge, and gently round over the eye. The cheek markings are simple cuts with the No. 11, U gouge.

Feet.—Round over the whole of each foot to form the side elevation shape, then make two cuts in each to separate the toes. Finally round over each toe individually.

The woodwork is completed by making sweeping cuts to form the wings, using the small U gouge. The breast wood is then eased down into it, so leaving the wings standing up. For the feathers run the small U gouge around the shape (pencil them in first), then ease away the waste with the flat gouge so that the feathers appear to lie one over the other.

Finish.—Colours can be taken from nature. That in Fig. 1 was in varying shades of red over head, lower breast, back, and rear part of wings. Top breast and front of wings in light blue with yellow markings. The most durable finish is artists' oil colours followed by varnish, but it takes a long time to dry —over a week. A very effective alternative is poster or show-card water colours. These are slightly diluted with water and are completely opaque. When dry follow with a coat of clear oil varnish. As a preliminary before painting it is as well to give a coat of gluesize as this prevents the varnish from sinking.

½ 7   ½ 3   ½ 4   **FIG. 6. THE TOOLS USED**
These were the shapes of the tools used in making the bird in Fig. 1. They could be varied within reasonable limits however.

½ 8   ¼ 5   ¼ 4   //

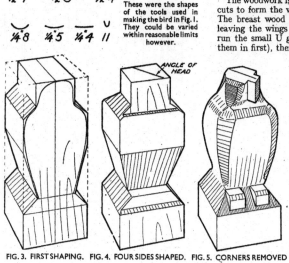

FIG. 3. FIRST SHAPING. FIG. 4. FOUR SIDES SHAPED. FIG. 5. CORNERS REMOVED

THE ACANTHUS LEAF

There are various ways of treating the acanthus leaf. In the conventional form in Fig. 1 the lobes are of a hollow section which makes for simplicity. A more naturalesque treatment is followed in Fig. 7 in which the lobes are mostly rounded.

FIG. I. ACANTHUS LEAF PANEL. Size 7 ins. by 5½ ins. by ⅞ in. Carving a leaf of this size and type not only forms an introduction to a widely used motif, but affords excellent practice in clean, crisp cutting. To the left the leaf is modelled before the smaller lobes are cut in.

ALTHOUGH not intended for the decoration of any particular item, the acanthus leaf in Fig. 1 could easily be adapted for the treatment of a book end, bracket, or the panel of a piece of furniture. Its chief purpose, however, is to introduce the reader to the general form and treatment of the leaf so that he may apply the experience he gains in cutting it to any variation of the leaf across which he may come.

The Drawing.—This is shown in full size in Fig. 2. Note that the small lobes are shown bounded by a thick line which embraces each group: For immediate purposes only this thick line is needed, though it is as well to put in the individual lobes so that their correct grouping is assured. Transfer the design (thick line only) to a piece of ⅞ in. wood by means of carbon paper. A centre line drawn along the wood will enable the half-drawing to be positioned exactly.

Before beginning any practical work study the drawing in Fig. 2, especially the section and the side view. Note first that the centre rib is at its highest about 1 in. from the bottom and falls away towards the top in an ogee shape (see side view). This is the general shape of the whole leaf, except for the pipes which stand up somewhat from the rest. Observe, too, that the centre is the thickest part, the lobes becoming thinner towards their tips. Finally, see how the leaf stands up from the background, the latter being cut away to a flat surface.

Setting In.—As the wood is ⅞ in. thick and the background finishes a full ¼ in., practically ⅝ in. of wood has to be removed all round the design. Set a gauge to the finished depth and mark round the edges of the panel. Fig. 3, A, shows the first stage of recessing the background. A fairly large, thick gouge, say a ½ in. No. 7, is worked around the outline about ⅛ in. from it, and the waste removed by cutting in from the edge. It is always easier to cut across the grain. Repeat the process until the groundwork is within about ⅛ in. of the finished depth.

Now, selecting gouges which approximate to the curve, set in the outline; that is to say, cut

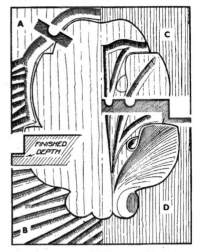

FIG. 3.
VARIOUS STAGES IN CARVING THE LEAF
A. Preliminary stage in recessing groundwork. B. Design set in and ground partly removed. C. Hollows cut around rib and pipes. D. Parts of leaf modelled and the eyes cut in.

16

WATCH CONTINUITY OF LINE IN THE DRAWING

down vertically all round, as at B, Fig. 3. A flatter gouge, such as a ½ in. No. 4, can be used for the surface of the groundwork. You will realise that the reason why the latter is stopped short of the finished depth (see section at B) is that the groundwork is bound to be marked somewhat by the setting in, and when the individual lobes are cut later, these marks can be removed. The purpose of making the cut around the outline as at A before setting in is to enable the wood to crumble away easily on the waste side. If this were not done the wedge shape of the gouge would offer considerable resistance to its being driven downwards. It might also have the effect of pressing it into the design.

It has already been noted that the general shape of the leaf when viewed from the side is an ogee curve. This shape has to be worked before the detail can be put in, but in order that the positions of the centre rib and the pipes may not be entirely lost (as they would be owing to the cutting away of the surface) a cut is made at each side of them with a large veiner (⅜ in. 11). The cuts should deepen towards the top where the wood is to be cut away most. This is shown clearly at C, Fig. 3, where an additional cut is also shown immediately beneath the turned-over top.

Bosting In.—In this the general contour of the leaf is worked before any detail is attempted. It is extremely important because the modelling and balance of the work depend largely upon it. To do without it would be like trying to cut detail upon the surface of a piece of rough, uneven wood which had not been planed.

Since the centre rib really controls the main shape of the leaf a start can be made on this, cutting it back to an ogee shape (see side view in Fig. 2). The advantage of having cut in the sides of the rib with the veiner is felt here. The rib will, of course, become wider as more wood is cut away owing to the rounded hollows

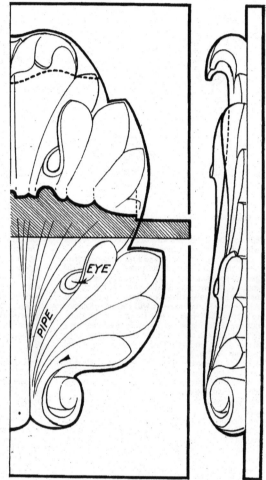

FIG 2. HALF PATTERN IN FULL SIZE. ALSO SIDE VIEW

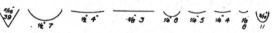

FULL SIZE SHAPES OF TOOLS USED IN CARVING THIS DESIGN

17

Good Form Is More Important Than Technique

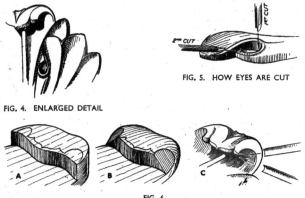

FIG. 4. ENLARGED DETAIL

FIG. 5. HOW EYES ARE CUT

FIG. 6.
STAGES IN WORKING TOP LEAF WHICH CURLS FORWARD AND IS HOLLOWED BENEATH

cut by the veiner, but this can be corrected later when the surface is modelled.

Now, using the ½ in. (4) and ¼ in. (8) gouges clear away the wood around the pipes, and form the general shape of the leaves. Remember the general contour (see section and side views in Fig. 2) and reduce the wood until it approximates to the shape. As the wood is cut away it will become necessary to deepen the veiner cuts, at the sides of the pipes, but avoid cutting in too deeply because they have to flow into the surface of the leaf. The eyes (Fig. 2) can also be cut in, the ⅛ in. No. 8 gouge being used as shown in Fig. 5.

D, Fig. 3, shows this bosting-in stage. Bear in mind that the leaves are thickest at the centre and become thin down at the tips. As the groundwork has to be cut away to the extent of another 1/16 in. or so, the edges of the leaves can approach the present level to within 1/16 in., this allowing sufficient wood for the modelling. When a leaf at one side has been finished, it is advisable to do the corresponding leaf on the other side so that the whole is balanced. The left hand side in Fig. 1 shows the work at this bosted-in stage.

Outlining and Modelling.—You can now sketch in the shape of the lobes, and the raised arrises formed by the hollow shapes. These arrises must be in an unbroken curve and flow naturally from the centre rib. They need be put in in pencil approximately only. The actual cutting enables any inaccuracies to be corrected. Selecting gouges to fit the various parts of the outline, cut down vertically all round the lobes. Cut in deeply where

the lobes lie on the background, but avoid cutting in too far where they overlap other lobes. Now reduce the background right down to the gauge line. Use the No. 4, ½ in. gouge first, and finish off with the No. 3, ⅝ in.

To form the hollow contour of the lobes the best plan is to use a quick gouge at the sides (¼ in., 8) and a flatter one for the centre. This makes the arrises or ridges well defined without removing too much wood in the middle. It is in this part of the work that the grain will prove something of a problem, and you will continually have to change the direction of the cut to avoid tearing out. The tools must be razor sharp, especially if working in a softwood across the grain. Note that the overlapping leaves fold down from the high wood around the eyes so that they appear to lie naturally. Where the hollows narrow towards the bottom the quick gouge only is used.

One other point is that the veiner is used for the outer sides of the pipes, but that the inner sides facing the centre rib are cut down vertically to an acute corner with a flat gouge and the surface of the lower leaf cut into it. The eyes will probably need further attention. The edge from the overlapping lobe slopes downward so that it appears to pass beneath itself. (See Fig. 4.)

Fig. 6 shows how the top leaf which curls forward is worked. A shows the flat wood with the lines marked in. At B the general surface is rounded over, and the corners are cut away at an angle. C. shows how the leaf is hollowed, a quick gouge being taken in from the sides.

Scrolls.—The last job is to model the scrolls at the base. Slope away the sides at an angle and then shape out the line of the scroll approximately with a fine veiner. Where the leaf joins the scroll the edge can be set in vertically, but the angle changes as the bottom is reached and has to slope into that of the centre boss. The latter is finished off by careful cutting in from the side, a gouge with its hollow side downward being used.

Naturalesque Leaf, Fig. 7.—Draw the leaf on paper, making sure that the parts spring naturally from each other, and make a tracing of the main

CUT MAIN FORM BEFORE PUTTING IN DETAILS

outline, omitting all smaller lobes. Transfer this to the wood with carbon paper. Decide the total relief and mark around the edges with a gauge. The leaf in Fig. 7 was carved in $\frac{7}{8}$ in. wood, and the groundwork was sunk $\frac{7}{16}$ in.

With a fairly large, quick gouge (say, $\frac{1}{2}$ in., No. 7) cut away the groundwork as in Fig. 8. Stop slightly short of the pencil line, and carry the surface down to about $\frac{1}{32}$ in. to $\frac{1}{16}$ in. of the gauge line. Do not bother to smooth it at this stage. Where the smaller lobes occur a smaller gouge can be used.

The general form of the leaf has

FIG. 7. SHAPELY AND WELL MODELLED ACAN-
THUS LEAF IN MAHOGANY
The acanthus leaf occurs in wood carving to a considerable extent. Apart from the outline shaping the modelling plays an important part. In cheap work the leaf is fretted and applied to the groundwork.

pencil marks as you work but this does not matter, they are easily sketched in again.

Finally cut down the outline of the lobes, using gouges to suit the varying curves. Slightly undercut to give a feeling of lightness and detachment. The groundwork is then cut down to the gauge right up to the leaf, a flat wide gauge being used. For awkward, sharp corners a narrow flat gouge is needed, and sometimes a side tool. It is an advantage slightly to chamfer the edges of the leaves as this makes them stronger.

FIG. 8.
PRELIMINARY SINKING OF THE GROUNDWORK
Note that the drawing at this early stage embraces only the main shape. Details of the leaf are not cut down until after the modelling.

now to be given. The highest part occurs just behind the turn-over of the leaf to the right. From this point the leaf should be gradually lowered to the left right down to the stalk. The same thing applies to the tip of the main leaf. Do not cut away the ridge behind the fork of the main and second leaves. This is somewhat lower than the other high point, but is higher than the rest of the surface. You can also cut down the lobe at the turn-over. Cut it down to the approximate shape, but do not attempt any detail until the whole has been bosted in. This part of the work is most important.

Now sketch in the detail of the lobes as in Fig. 9. This will be a guide to the modelling which now follows. Keep the various hollows and rounds running in long continuous sweeps without disjointedness. You will remove the

FIG. 9. FIRST STAGE IN THE SURFACE MODELLING
The leaf outline is sketched in as a guide to how the modelling is carried out. The gradual taper from the high parts to the low are worked first before details are put in.

19

FIG. I.
FINE PANEL DATING FROM THE EARLY 16TH CENTURY
It will be seen that the folds do actually appear to fold over each other, the modelling at top and bottom emphasizing this.

THERE are many kinds of linenfold panels, some simple, others elaborate. Some, although coming under the general heading of linenfold, are really little more than vertical ridges with the ends treated in a decorative fashion. The true linenfold actually shows the folds of a piece of linen lying one over the other, and the ends at top and bottom emphasize this as in the example in Fig. 1.

Drawing.—Draw in the design on paper in elevation and show the end view. The latter is important because it shows not only the section, but also the actual folds of the linen. This may sound a little obvious, but you will realize its value when you come to the actual work, remembering that the ends have to be recessed to different levels in accordance with how the folds happen to lie over each other. Fig. 2 shows the sort of drawing to prepare.

Working the Folds.—From the end view in Fig. 2 you can see at once the section (heavy line) to which the panel has to be worked. You

CARVING THE
LINENFOLD
PANEL

This linenfold panel is taken from one in the pulpit in the nave of Westminster Abbey. It is a specially fine example in that it does actually resemble (in conventional form) the folds of a linen cloth. It makes a delightful motif for a piece of early English woodwork.

can do this almost entirely with the plough, rebate plane, and various moulding planes, though certain parts (the quirk marked X, for instance) will have to be finished with carving tools owing to the pointed shape. Fig. 3 shows to the left the preliminary cuts made with the plough ; the other half shows the finished shape. Those parts needing to be undercut are left straight down at this stage, the undercutting being best done later. Some workers do the whole of the general shaping of the wood with carving tools, but it is a laborious job requiring considerable skill to retain the folds in correct section throughout their length.

Recessing the Groundwork.—We now have the panel finished up to the stage shown in Fig. 4, the rebate at the sides being continued round at top and bottom as far in as the design. You have now to cut away all wood which lies beyond the actual linenfold down as far as the groundwork, and you will probably be surprised to find that these do not seem to line up with the ridges and folds of the panel. The reason for this, of course, is that the lines you are drawing in represent the back folds, whilst the vertical ridges are the front ones. However, if you draw in the complete folds it will become more obvious. It is a little more difficult than it sounds because of the undulating shape, but you can measure down at various points and mark accordingly. Fig. 5 shows one end marked, the actual outline being drawn in heavily.

One point to note is that in the drawing of the front folds the curves do not flow directly out of each other, but start a little way in. For instance, in the enlarged detail in Fig. 5, the line X curves down into the rear vertical member. The next one Y, which really continues the fold forwards, starts a little way in and runs to the next vertical member. The same thing applies to Z, and so on. This is because a certain thickness must be allowed at the edges of the wood, a detail which will become more obvious later. An experienced carver, from long experience, knows details such as this, and his marking out is far more sketchy. A check with rule or dividers at various points is all he needs. For the rest he judges with his eye whether the parts are balanced.

20

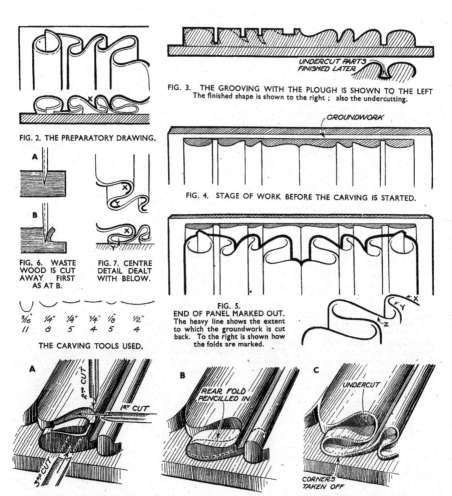

FIG. 2. THE PREPARATORY DRAWING.

FIG. 3. THE GROOVING WITH THE PLOUGH IS SHOWN TO THE LEFT
The finished shape is shown to the right ; also the undercutting.

UNDERCUT PARTS
FINISHED LATER

GROUNDWORK

FIG. 4. STAGE OF WORK BEFORE THE CARVING IS STARTED.

A

B

FIG. 6. WASTE
WOOD IS CUT
AWAY FIRST
AS AT B.

FIG. 7. CENTRE
DETAIL DEALT
WITH BELOW.

FIG. 5.
END OF PANEL MARKED OUT.
The heavy line shows the extent
to which the groundwork is cut
back. To the right is shown how
the folds are marked.

3/16	1/4"	1/4"	1/4"	1/8	1/2"
11	8	5	4	5	4

THE CARVING TOOLS USED.

A 2ND CUT 1ST CUT 3RD CUT

B REAR FOLD PENCILLED IN

C UNDERCUT CORNERS TAKEN OFF

FIG. 8. VARIOUS STAGES IN WORKING THE PORTION SHOWN IN FIG. 7. THE OTHER PARTS ARE CARVED SIMILARLY.

Carving the Ends.—Now if you were to cut down vertically with gouges and mallet straightway you would find it a laborious task. In parts you would have to chop down as much as $\frac{1}{2}$ in., and you might easily snap off the point of the gouge. Furthermore, the wedge shape of the gouge edge would offer great resistance and tend to press into

the design. A in Fig. 6 makes this clear.

The plan is therefore adopted of cutting away a great deal of the waste first with a quick gouge. It can be removed up to within about $\frac{1}{16}$ in. or $\frac{1}{8}$ in. Then the wood will crumble away easily on the waste side and there will be no tendency for the

(Continued on page 24.)

RENAISSANCE DESIGN FOR
BELLOWS

The front of a pair of bellows makes an interesting subject to carve. The design in Fig. 1 is in ½ in. oak with the background recessed to a depth of 3/16 in. It is intended to have a separate handle screwed on. If preferred, however, the handle could be cut out in one piece with the front. Incidentally, full instructions on making the bellows appear in HOME HOBBIES IN WOOD, *a companion to this book.*

of work, and, carried out in oak, looks most attractive. As shown in Fig. 1 it is intended to have a separate handle. Some, however, may prefer to form a handle in the same piece of wood, in which case an additional length of 4½-5 ins. should be allowed.

Transferring the Design.—First make a tracing of the design in Fig. 2. Prepare the wood to the required size and draw in a centre line. To transfer the pattern place it on the wood so that the two centre lines coincide, and slip a piece of carbon paper beneath. By going carefully over every line the pattern can be marked out clearly. A couple of drawing pins can be used to hold the paper steady, these being pushed into parts of the wood which are to be cut away. The main outer shape can then be cut out with the saw and finished off with the plane. The bullnose plane will be handy for smoothing near the bottom. The spokeshave will also come in.

Outlining.—Now for the carving. The whole design has to be set in—that is,

FIG. I.
ATTRACTIVE COMBINATION OF STRAP AND LEAF WORK
The size of the design is 10⅝ ins. by 9 ins. Conventional leaf work and interlacing straps were frequently used in the Renaissance carving of the 16th and 17th centuries.

THE design in Fig. 1 is founded on the Renaissance style. It shows typical features in the use of the interlacing strapwork and the conventional leaves. It is a straightforward and comparatively simple piece

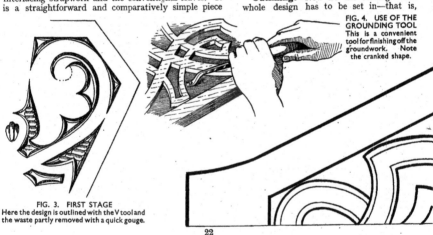

FIG. 4. USE OF THE GROUNDING TOOL
This is a convenient tool for finishing off the groundwork. Note the cranked shape.

FIG. 3. FIRST STAGE
Here the design is outlined with the V tool and the waste partly removed with a quick gouge.

YOU SAVE TIME BY OUTLINING THE DESIGN FIRST

downward cuts have to be made all round the various outlines. To do this straightway, however, would involve a great deal of hard chopping, necessitating the use of the mallet, and there would be the risk of the gouge edge splintering away. The better plan is to run around the outlines with the V tool, this being kept always on the waste side. Then, when the setting in is being done, the wood will crumble away on the waste side as the gouge is pressed down into the wood. The exact size of V tool used does not matter much, but select a fairly large one—say, $\frac{5}{16}$ in., No. 39.

Keep it on the waste side of the line and endeavour to work it in long cuts. You will not be able to take it around the quicker curves or acute corners, but then there is no need to. At the top, for instance, you will see that no attempt is made to cut the hollow shape of the top leaf (it is shown by the dotted line in Fig. 3 which shows the V tooling). The waste wood of a curve like this is best loosened with a quick gouge. One point to note is that at sharply-pointed corners where the grain runs crosswise, it is advisable to work the tool *into* the corner rather than *away from* it. The latter would probably tend to make the point split away.

Sinking the Groundwork.—At this stage a great deal of waste can be cut away with a quick gouge, say, $\frac{1}{4}$ in., No. 8. This is shown in the lower part of Fig. 3. If worked across the grain the work will be easier and there will be no liability for the gouge to drift with the grain. No attempt is made at a smooth finish—this follows later. All you are doing now is to remove the bulk of the waste (it is rather like the holes you bore in a mortise before you begin to use the chisel). Be sure to keep the groundwork above the finished depth of $\frac{3}{16}$ in. In the case of some of the smaller recesses you will probably find it impossible to use the V tool to any extent. But it does not matter. Remember that its sole purpose is to ease the setting-in. All you need do is to cut away as much as you can with a quick gouge.

Setting In.—When chopping down with gouges select tools which fit the particular part of the curve you are cutting. Discretion is needed because in many cases you will not have a gouge which exactly fits the shape. In the nature of things this is bound to be so because the gouges are shaped to arcs of circles whereas many of the curves are elliptical. The rule to adopt is to use a rather quicker gouge for concave shapes, and a flatter one for convex curves. This avoids digging in the corners. Take special care at outer corners in which the grain runs crosswise—some of the leaf points, for instance. Work from the weak corner towards the wider stronger part. Otherwise you may break them off.

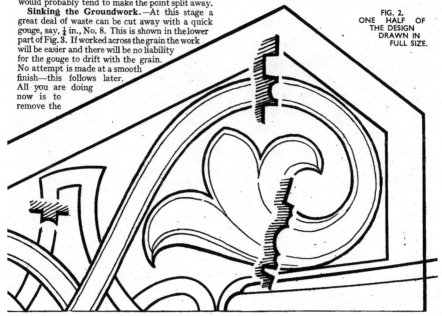

FIG. 2.
ONE HALF OF THE DESIGN DRAWN IN FULL SIZE.

BACKGROUND MUST BE RECESSED TO EQUAL DEPTH

You can still to an extent use an ordinary straight, flat gouge for lowering the groundwork—at any rate, in the larger recesses. · For the greater

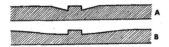

FIG. 5. INTERLACING THE STRAPS
Avoid the sudden dip at A. Rather let the slope be gradual as at B.

part, however, the cranked grounding tool is needed. It is used as shown in Fig. 4. Use a wide one where possible—say, $\frac{1}{4}$ in.—as this is better for producing a flat surface, but for corners you will need a narrow one, preferably with the edge askew.

Interlacing and Modelling.—You will see from Fig. 1 that certain of the straps appear to pass beneath the others. This effect is obtained by gently lowering the surface with a flat gouge (say, $\frac{1}{4}$ in., No. 3). It is important that the lowering is gradual. The effect at A, Fig. 5, for example, is quite useless. Strive for that at B, beginning the slope well back from where it passes beneath the other strap.

Note that the broad straps have a hollow in the centre, leaving a narrow square at each side. Use a $\frac{1}{4}$ in., No. 8 gouge for this, and endeavour to work

in long, even cuts. It is necessary to work the tool then in the direction which best suits the side of the hollow you are finishing. If you prefer you can pencil in lines as a guide, using the finger as a gauge. It is not essential, however, as it can be judged by the eye. In the narrow straps the hollow is taken right across the width.

Leaves.—Fig. 6 shows how the leaves are carved. At the sides of the hollows use the quick gouge ($\frac{1}{4}$ in., No. 8) and in the centre the flatter gouge ($\frac{1}{4}$ in., No. 5). This applies to the wider leaves.

FIG. 6. DETAIL OF THE LEAVES
A quick gouge is used at the sides and a flat one for the centre.

Once again work the tool in the direction which best suits the grain. Keep the hollows a full $\frac{1}{16}$ in. from the edges, and finish off by chamfering the last named. Use a flat gouge and run it around the edges in bold sweeps.

LINENFOLD PANEL (*continued from page 21*)

gouge to press into the design (see B, Fig. 6).

One last point. It is inevitable when the modelling of the folds is done later that the outline will have to be corrected and trimmed. It is therefore advisable to work about $\frac{1}{32}$ in. short of the line when cutting down (setting in, as it is called). For the same reason you can stop a trifle short of the finished depth. Bearing this in mind take care to avoid chopping too deeply with the gouges, because this creates unsightly marks which are difficult to remove.

Modelling.—We now come to the modelling of the folds, and when you do this always keep in mind the natural way the folds lie when viewed from the end. As an actual example take the small centre portion shown in Fig. 7. With a quick gouge (say, $\frac{1}{4}$ in. No. 8) waste away the wood nearly up to the line as shown by the first cut in Fig. 8, A. Then with the same gouge make a vertical cut at X (see second cut). With other flatter gouges work towards the centre, selecting gouges which fit the curve as nearly as possible. The third cut is horizontal from the end (see A, Fig. 8) and this models the work to the folds as far as possible. The net result of these three cuts· is the rough

resemblance to the modelling shown at B.

You will realize that in cutting back the first fold X, the line of the second fold Y has necessarily been lost. This must now be pencilled in and the second fold Y cut similarly to the first. To obtain a realistic effect, however, it is necessary to undercut the work, and this is now done. At the same time any truing up of the line is carried out. The undercutting of the actual vertical folds can also be done. The simplest way of doing this is to draw a skew chisel straight along the angle.

Corners.—The most awkward part of the work is in taking out cleanly the acute curves such as X. As in all carving every chip of wood must be *cut* cleanly away. Scraping away with the edge of the tool cannot provide a clean finish. The only way is to cut downwards and then horizontally. One of the troubles is that, owing to the undercutting, the gouge has to be taken in deeply, and if the $\frac{1}{4}$ in. gouge is used the outer corner is liable to make an unsightly mark. To overcome this a $\frac{1}{8}$ in. gouge of the same curvature should be used to finish off. This can be used in the deep parts without touching the higher portions.

To finish off, the edges of the folds are taken off at about 45 degrees.

TRAY
with early
GOTHIC
CARVING

The full-size design given on page 26 can be repeated at all four corners, or, better still, it can be varied with the same general character retained. A photograph of a tray with the four corners carved in different detail is given on page 46.

THE tray shown in Fig. 1 measures 2 ft. ¾ ins. by 15¾ ins. overall, and consists of a base-board of ½ in. oak with an edging fixed to it with screws driven upwards from beneath. It will probably be necessary to joint

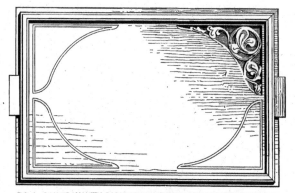

FIG. I. OAK TRAY WITH CARVING FOUNDED ON EARLY ENGLISH GOTHIC
Although in the ordinary way it is not advisable to carve the surface of a tray owing to the liability of glasses, etc., to be upset when placed upon an uneven surface, it is quite in order in the present case since it is proposed to fit a sheet of glass inside the edging.

together two pieces to obtain the width, and it is advisable to cut them from the same board so that the grain is matched as far as possible. A plain rubbed joint can be used. Having made the joint, cleaned up the surface, and squared the edges to size, centre lines should be drawn along the length and across the width. Lines giving the position at the edging are also needed.

THE DRAWING
Marking Out. —Make a tracing of Fig. 7; and from this transfer the design to the wood by means of carbon paper.

You will realize that the design consists of a main scroll and conventional leaves standing up from a recessed groundwork (Fig. 7). The latter is taken in to a depth of at least ¼ in. (⁵⁄₁₆ in. would give better opportunity for modelling), and the edges are bevelled where they meet the main surface of the tray. Along the centre of each main lobe runs a raised centre part, both this and the lobes themselves being rounded in shape. A study of Fig. 7 makes this clear. The sections in this are taken at right angles with the general flow of the design, and this forms a useful way of giving sections known as the rectangular system. You will realize

FIG. 3. GROUNDWORK SUNK BEFORE MODELLING

FIG. 2. FIRST STAGE SHOWING OUTLINING WITH V TOOL

FIG. 4. THE GROUNDING TOOL SHOWING CRANKED SHAPE

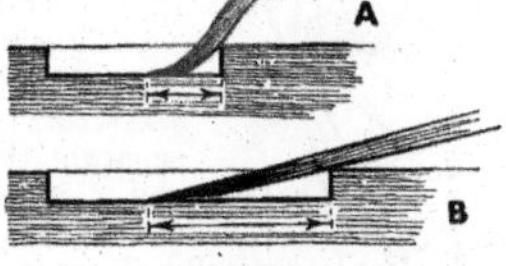

FIG. 5. HOW GROUNDING TOOL CAN BE USED IN SMALL RECESSES

GROUNDING TOOLS

FIG. 6. TOOLS USED IN CARVING THE OAK TRAY

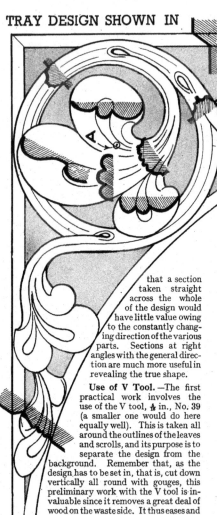

FIG. 7. FULL-SIZE DESIGN
FOR TRAY CORNER

that a section taken straight across the whole of the design would have little value owing to the constantly changing direction of the various parts. Sections at right angles with the general direction are much more useful in revealing the true shape.

Use of V Tool. —The first practical work involves the use of the V tool, 𝟷𝟼 in., No. 39 (a smaller one would do here equally well). This is taken all around the outlines of the leaves and scrolls, and its purpose is to separate the design from the background. Remember that, as the design has to be set in, that is, cut down vertically all round with gouges, this preliminary work with the V tool is invaluable since it removes a great deal of wood on the waste side. It thus eases and simplifies the later stages of the work. You will not be able to follow the smaller intricacies of the design, especially in the more acute curves and corners, but it is with the main sweeps that you are mostly concerned. At the same time that you are using this V tool you can make a cut at each

side of the centre raised part in each lobe. This marks their positions and gives a start in the later modelling process. Fig. 2 shows the work at this stage. The section at B shows the V cuts clearly. Note specially that the cuts *on* the leaves are shallower than those at the edges. The last named should be fairly deep because the background has to be recessed at least ½ in. Do not attempt to take the tool right down to the finished depth, however.

When working at an angle across the grain you will find that one side of the V tool is liable to tear out the grain whilst the other leaves it perfectly clean. You have therefore to consider which is the best direction in which to work it. One side of the cut is important whilst the other does not matter. You must therefore work in the direction which gives a clean finish to the side that matters. Take, for instance, the portion at A, Fig. 2. It is clear that the tool should be worked in the direction shown by the arrow because the left-hand side of the V will give a clean finish to the stem. The right-hand side which is liable to tear out is only part of the background which has to be cut away.

Incidentally, the keener the cutting edge the less liable it is to tear out—in fact, a really keen carving tool can often be taken against the grain without tearing out, providing that only thin chips are removed. There are, indeed, occasions on which the only way the tool can be used is against the grain, and this is when a razor-like edge is essential.

Sinking the Groundwork.—Now follows the setting-in and recessing of the groundwork. Selecting gouges which fit the shape, work all round the outline of the lobes and scrolls, stopping, however, at places where the first named overlap the scrolls. Hold the tools so that an upright cut is made. You will probably not take the tool down to the finished depth in one cut; you will have to remove some of the groundwork and then cut down again. In any case, stop short of the finished depth because the work is bound to need correction and cleaning up later, and it would not do to leave unsightly tool marks.

A certain amount of waste can be removed with an ordinary straight gouge, but to finish cleanly you will need a bent chisel or grounding tool, as it is called (see Fig. 4). This can be used in recesses of much smaller size as Fig. 5 makes clear. For the wider spaces a No. 25, $\frac{1}{4}$ in. size is suitable, and a $\frac{1}{8}$ in. for smaller ones. You will also need a $\frac{1}{8}$ in. left-corner grounding tool for getting closely into acute corners. This is similar to the tool shown in Fig. 4 but the edge is sharpened askew. Fig. 3 shows the appearance of the work when the background has been recessed.

Modelling.—In the modelling which follows observe the sections in Fig. 7 and work *with* the grain as far as possible. It may mean that a cut will have to be started in one direction and finished in the other owing to the changing direction. On this score note that it is a tremendous advantage to be able to work with either hand. It saves having to release the wood and turn it round. Endeavour to work in long, deliberate cuts and avoid little niggling chips. You won't attain perfection straightway, but it is a technique for which to strive. This is particularly the case when modelling the scrolls in which the facets should run in long, unbroken sweeps.

For a start you can round over the scrolls, using the No. 5, $\frac{1}{4}$ in., gouge with the hollow side downwards, and put in the hollows afterwards with the No. 5, $\frac{3}{8}$-in., gouge. For the small eyes where the scrolls branch from each other, make a downward stab with the small veiner, No. 11, $\frac{1}{16}$ in., and cut the long sides with the Nos. 5 and 4, $\frac{1}{4}$ in. gouges. The narrow grounding tool will remove the waste chip.

The ends of the raised portions of the lobes are cut vertically with a gouge which fits the shape. Then, by holding the tool low down with the hollow side downwards the rounded shape can be given. Start about $\frac{1}{8}$ in. or so back from the downward cut, and as the tool moves forward raise the handle so that the horizontal cut changes to an upright one. For the long sides use gouges which fit the shape and work in long strokes with the hollow side downwards. Be careful to avoid digging in the corners.

Note that immediately in front of the raised centre the lobe is hollowed. This can be put in with the $\frac{1}{4}$ in. No. 8 gouge and the edges sloped away with flatter gouges.

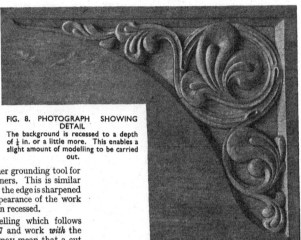

FIG. 8. PHOTOGRAPH SHOWING DETAIL
The background is recessed to a depth of $\frac{1}{4}$ in. or a little more. This enables a slight amount of modelling to be carried out.

SWAG OF FRUIT AND FLOWERS
(continued from page 31)

of the line in every case. Take, for instance, the husk adjoining the knot. The veiner is taken just outside so that the line is left in.

The bosting stage is completed by forming the individual details a little more closely. This is shown to the left in Fig. 2, where the knot of the ribbon is made to stand out, and the drapery sloped in beneath it. The interior spaces of the ribbons are taken out and their general undulating form cut. The fruit and floral items are separated and roughly modelled to their final form. As you do this you will find that you will have to cut in the outline more accurately, but do not stab down to the full depth until you are sure of the final form. Remember that some of the items present a side or three-quarter view instead of front view.

Modelling.—The last stage is shown to the left in Fig. 1. The shape of each item is rounded or modelled to its final form and its outline cut in cleanly. The tool will have to work whichever way is the most convenient for the grain, but frequently the direction can help the design. For instance, in the flower the tool marks radiate. Do not make each leaf or petal a replica of its neighbour. It isn't so in nature. Rather give them a twist or turn, just as happens in the real thing. Throughout the work remember to model in the main form before putting in detail. In the drapery, for example, model the main folds first and add the smaller local detail afterwards.

27

BOOK ENDS
WITH PIERCED DESIGN

This is an interesting piece of work in that wood is pierced right through. To an extent the work is lessened since the saw can be used to remove much of the waste. On the other hand, the modelling is deep.

FIG. 1. EXAMPLE OF CONVENTIONAL LEAFWORK
The larger openings in this design are pierced right through. The scroll or coping saw is used for this. Main sizes are 7 ins. high, 5¼ ins. wide, and 4 ins. deep.

THE main upright is seen on one side only, and the inner side which faces the books is merely bevelled off. The bracket is seen on both sides, and must be finished off equally well on both.

Walnut, perhaps, is first choice, but oak is very effective. If the whole seems somewhat light a metal plate can be added to the bottom on which the first two books can rest. For the uprights and brackets ¾ in. finished stuff is used, the base being ⅞ in. thick. A slight variation would not matter much.

The Drawing.—Trace Fig. 2 and transfer to the wood by means of carbon paper. One half being done, the paper can be reversed and the rest completed.

The pierced portions are shown shaded in Fig. 2, and it is necessary to bore holes as shown by the black circles to enable the saw to be started. The most satisfactory is a scroll saw, which is like a strong and thick fretsaw. If care is taken the cut can be made practically up to the line.

Before beginning the carving the joint between the upright and the base should be cut. This can conveniently be a lapped dovetail. The bracket needs only to be butted since it is screwed upwards through the base, and through from the inside of the upright.

The V Tool.—The preliminary cuts are made with a fairly large V tool—say, a ⅜ in. tool, though the exact size does not matter. Study the section of the design and start the tool either to one side of the line or right on it, according to the section required. Note, too, that in some cases it will be an advantage to hold it at an angle so that one side of the cut is upright or practically so.

Modelling.—Now, observing the section in Fig. 2, cut away the wood of the main leaves so that they are rounded or hollowed as may be required. For the rounded members a gouge, say, ¼ in., 4 or 5, can be used with the hollow side downwards. Where one leaf scrolls over another ease away the waste first with a fairly quick gouge—a ³⁄₁₆ in., 9, is handy. The cut down with gouges of appropriate curvature—¼ in., Nos. 4 and 5, are invaluable. In the case of the bottom scroll cut down vertically, starting at the centre boss, changing the gouge as may be required—for the extreme centre you will need a ⅛ in., No. 7—and slope away the waste to meet it at the bottom.

Fig. 4 shows how the tips of the leaves are managed. A shows the leaf approximately modelled and a cut with a quick gouge made around the right-hand side. With a flat gouge—the ½ in., No. 4, will do—cut away the leaf to the dotted line. Then using the ¼ in., No. 5, cut down as shown by the top gouge and remove the waste as shown by the bottom one. Now take the quicker No. 7 gouge, make a cut at the right, starting vertically but leaning the handle over to the right as the cut deepens. This will produce the effect shown at B.

In this way go over the whole design until all is modelled. Work with long crisp cuts, making their direction emphasize the design. For instance, the cuts should be along the direction of the leaves. Don't try to take out all tool marks—you are not trying to produce a glasspapered effect. Cleaning the sides of the saw cuts is an awkward but necessary job. Use appropriately curved gouges and cut down on to a flat board.

The Back.—At the back the openings should be lightly chamfered as in Fig. 5. To make the corners neat make a mitre cut right in every corner and slope away the waste at each side of it. In this way perfectly clean corners can be produced.

28

FULL SIZE DESIGN AND STAGES IN CARVING

FIG. 6. TOOLS USED IN CUTTING THE DESIGN

FIG. 3. USING V TOOL.

FIG. 4.
HOW TO CUT TIPS OF LEAVES

FIG. 5.
OPENING FROM BACK SHOWING CHAMFERING OF EDGES

FIG. 2.
(right)
FULL SIZE DESIGN OF BRACKET AND UPRIGHT

A

B

FIG. I. SWAG DESIGN WITH ONE HALF OF WORK COMPLETED

Carving of this kind would be suitable for the decoration of a piece of Chippendale furniture. The grain of mahogany is often rather difficult and calls for razor-sharp tools.

SWAG
OF FRUIT
AND FLOWERS

This motif was used frequently in 18th century woodwork, and those who go in for woodwork of that period will find it a useful detail with which to be familiar. In good work it is cut in the solid (as here) but nowadays the usual plan is fret the outline, carve it, and apply to the work. This saves the laborious job of cutting the groundwork right back. Quite an appreciable amount of modelling is involved. The carving in Fig. 1 is in mahogany. The grain of this is often tricky, but is the wood in which most of this work was carried out.

THE carving in Fig. 1 is cut in a panel 9 ins. by 6½ ins., the thickness being ⅞ in., reduced to ⁵⁄₁₆ in. when the groundwork is lowered. The design could, of course, be cut on a piece of any size larger than this, such as a drawer front, frieze, or whatever it may be. Note that if it is proposed to fret out and apply the carving, it must be glued to a waste block of wood whilst the carving is being carried out. A piece of newspaper between the two enables the carving to be removed easily. The required thickness in this case is clearly ⁹⁄₁₆ in., though if it is a little more it will not hurt.

Drawing.—A study of Fig. 3 reveals that the highest part of the work is in the middle, the ends tapering where the greatest projection from the groundwork is no more than ¼ in. Clearly, then, it would be of no use carefully to draw in all the detail because it would immediately be removed at the first few chips. All you need is a drawing of the main outline so that you can sink

the background. Trace this from Fig. 3 and transfer to the wood with carbon paper. Gauge all round the depth to which the back-ground has to be lowered.

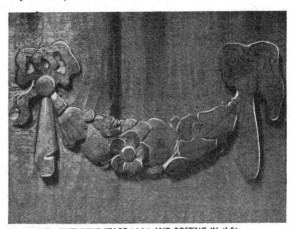

FIG. 2. OUTLINING STAGE (*right*) **AND BOSTING IN** (*left*)

The outlining is done after the wood has been sloped from the highest point (centre of the swag) towards the sides (see Fig. 3 A). It prevents the detail of the drawing from being lost entirely.

30

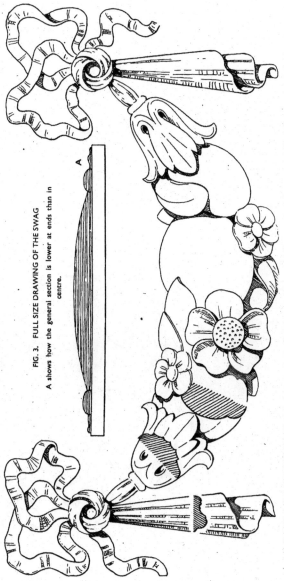

FIG. 3. FULL SIZE DRAWING OF THE SWAG

A shows how the general section is lower at ends than in centre.

Sinking the Background.—

Use a fairly large U-shaped tool to go around the outline. Leave a generous margin outside the line—say, $\frac{1}{16}$ in., and do not attempt to follow the line in detail. All you want is a guide to the masses of wood to be left. Take the tool down to within about $\frac{1}{16}$ in. of the finished depth.

To remove the waste use a fairly quick gouge for a start (the corners are not liable to dig in). It is generally an advantage to work across the grain, as the work is easier and the grain is not liable to split. Work down to within $\frac{1}{16}$ in. of the gauge line, substituting a flatter gouge as this depth is reached.

Bosting in.—You have now to make the whole thing conform to the general level of being highest at the middle and sinking to about $\frac{1}{2}$ in. at each end. Mark down along the outer edge of the ribbons and drapery the depth to which it has to be sunk. With a fairly flat, wide gouge ease away the wood towards the ends so that it takes the general form shown at A, Fig. 3. Keep the curve easy and gradual. So far as the centre swag is concerned, this is also rounded in sections across its width, and you can therefore take off the corners and round off the surface to an approximation of the final form.

On the surface so formed the detailed drawing is transferred. So far as the ribbons are concerned there is no difficulty since the surface is practically flat.

It is rather more awkward in the swag portion owing to the roundness. The best plan is to mark leading points from the tracing and then draw in the chief parts freehand. The tracing will form a general guide. It is, of course, inevitable that the removal of wood removes the drawing with it. To prevent its being entirely lost the main lines are put in with a small veiner as shown to the right in Fig. 2. Note that the veiner is taken on the waste side

(Continued on page 27.)

PANEL

Quite considerable experience is needed to make a good job of this panel. As shown here it is cut in oak, a hard if pleasant wood to cut. An alternative would be walnut or lime. In softwood it would be very difficult.

FIG. 1. ATTRACTIVE DESIGN FOR AN OAK PANEL
This is the most elaborate and most difficult design in the whole book, and should not be undertaken as a first effort. Being cut in to a depth of $\frac{7}{16}$ ins., considerable modelling is possible.

IT will be realized that the sprays and leaves undulate considerably, some of the oak leaves, for instance, being very low on the groundwork, whilst some of the laurel leaves are high. It follows then that the general bosting-in is desirable before much of the inner groundwork is sunk. Otherwise you will have a lot of awkward spaces to cut away without any advantage. At the same time it is clearly desirable for the groundwork to be taken back to the same depth throughout. To ensure this the larger internal openings should be cut—not in detail, but in general form. Unless this is done you will have no means of gauging the depth once the surface has been made to undulate.

Drawing.—Make a tracing of Fig. 2 and transfer the outline to the wood with carbon paper. The outlines of the internal openings you propose to cut should also be marked. No other detail need be put in, except that a note should be made of the high parts which will not have to be cut away.

Sinking the Groundwork.—This has to be cut away to a depth of $\frac{7}{16}$ in., and this size should be gauged around the edge. Run around the outline with a U tool, not attempting to follow the detail, but giving the general form. The same thing applies to the inner openings. Remove the waste wood with a large round gouge, working across the grain

FIG. 2. FULL-SIZE DRAWING OF THE DESIGN   NOTE THAT

32

WITH SPRAYS OF OAK AND LAUREL

where practicable, partly because it is easier, and partly because it avoids splitting. Take down to within about ¹⁄₁₆ in. of the finished depth. For the inner openings a small router can be used to ensure all being of the same depth throughout.

Bosting-In.—You have now to reduce the wood in the low parts to give the necessary undulations. For example, the laurel sprays are lowest at the knot and rise towards the first leaves. From this point they gradually drop until at the ends they are practically down to the background level. The oak sprays are lower, the highest point being the stalk midway between the two bunches of leaves. You can in a general way reduce the wood to follow the general scheme, and for this you need only an outline of the chief masses. As an instance, you clearly require to know the position of the oak stem because it is high at about midway of the length, whereas the leaves at each side are low. You should therefore pencil in the stalks; also

the acorns, which require a fair amount of thickness.

Having reduced the general surface in this way you can transfer the drawing in greater detail, giving the main masses. When you come actually to work it, however, do not feel too tied in by the drawing. You may feel that by shifting a leaf it may lie more naturally or gracefully, and you should not hesitate to do this—though never make this an excuse for bad workmanship.

The first necessity is to cut in an approximation of the general outline of the masses of leaves, berries, stalks, etc. Do not attempt to give the details. Just leave a broad mass for each bunch of leaves, etc. Cut round with a U or V tool. Sink the background so as to free the surface of all unnecessary detail. You now know within a little where the details are, and can carry the work to the fuller stage of modelling the individual masses of detail.

(Continued on page 43.)

THE SECTIONS SHOWN ARE GENERALLY TAKEN AT RIGHT ANGLES WITH THE GENERAL DIRECTION OF THE DETAIL

FIG. I. TYPICAL SINGLE-TWIST LEG
Apart from the obvious usefulness of being able to
make a twist leg it is a most fascinating job to do.

CARVING THE
TWIST LEG

*In normal times few would bother about
making twist legs: they can be obtained
ready made so easily. To-day, however, it is
a different matter, and we all have to do jobs
which would have been unnecessary a few
years ago. Possibly it may come as a surprise
to some that twist legs can be made perfectly
well without a lathe. If you have the latter it
certainly rather simplifies matters, but it is
not essential and you can in fact make a
better leg than the cheap commercial variety.*

IT may interest readers to know that the best twist-turned
legs are still a combination of turning and carving, and
that when they were first made in the 17th century the
lathe played a quite secondary part in the manufacture.
Here we assume that you have no lathe at all and are going
to rely upon normal hand woodworking tools plus one or
two carver's gouges.

Rounding the Wood.—Prepare your wood in the form
of a square as in Fig. 3, and mark in the centres at both
ends with the gauge. Continue the lines along the length
of the wood as shown, using a pencil. Mark in circles at the
ends, using dividers, and plane off the corners so that the
square is reduced to an octagon as in Fig. 4. Finally take
off the remaining corners, so rounding it, leaving the pencil
lines untouched.

Pitch.—We have now the pitch and depth of the twist to
consider. When a nut is revolved upon a bolt it rises by a
certain amount at each complete revolution. That is its
pitch, and a similar idea applies in a twist leg. Glance at A,
Fig. 2. The rounded part of the twist at the top of the
arrow passes spiralwise round the leg and when it reaches
a point vertically beneath it has completed one revolution,
and the distance down it has travelled is the pitch. There
is no definite ruling about it, but generally the pitch is made
to equal the diameter of the wood as in the present example.
You can vary it, however, by way of experiment if you
prefer.

Now for depth. The hollowed-out groove of the spiral
can be cut in so deeply that it passes more than halfway
through the wood, as at B, Fig. 2. This would be graceful
enough, but would have little strength and would be so
impracticable for most jobs. On the other hand, it could

be shallow as at C, in which case it would
appear as little more than an indetermin-
ate ripple along the surface. Obviously,
something between the two is needed, and
you can take into account the work the leg
is expected to do. For instance, a heavy
chair or table leg would have to be
shallower than a spindle, which carries no
weight. This depth, by the way, does not
affect the pitch.

Marking the Spiral.—We will assume
that the pitch is to equal the diameter,
and the next step must be to make a series
of rings round the leg, their distance apart
equalling the pitch. Thus, assuming the
diameter to be $1\frac{1}{2}$ ins., the distance between
AB, BC, etc. (Fig. 5), will be $1\frac{1}{2}$ ins. The
rings are easily drawn by wrapping a piece
of thin card with a straight edge around
the wood as shown.

To mark the spiral, take a length of
thin card having one edge perfectly
straight and, holding the true edge at the
point A, wrap it spiral-wise around the
leg, adjusting the position so that it cuts
the point B, then C, and so on as in Fig. 6.
A drawing-pin can be used to hold the end
temporarily. Run a pencil around the
straight edge so marking in the centre of
the rounded or high part of the twist.

Now turn to Fig. 5. You will see that
AB, BC, etc., are divided into quarters,
1, 2, 3. Actually, only the points 1, 3 are
needed, but 2 is marked in because it is
convenient to divide up into halves first.
Using the length of thin card again, wrap
it again round the leg to pass through the
points 1-1, etc., thus being parallel with
the first line. Repeat the process, this
time making the line cut the points 3-3,
etc. You thus have three distinct spirals

34

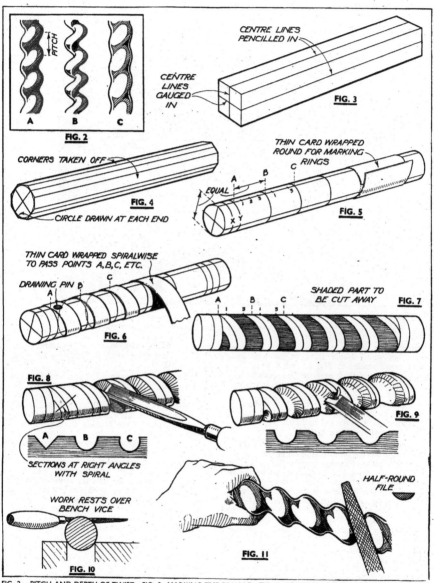

FIG. 2

CENTRE LINES PENCILLED IN

CENTRE LINES GAUGED IN

FIG. 3

CORNERS TAKEN OFF

CIRCLE DRAWN AT EACH END

FIG. 4

THIN CARD WRAPPED ROUND FOR MARKING RINGS

EQUAL

FIG. 5

THIN CARD WRAPPED SPIRALWISE TO PASS POINTS A,B,C, ETC.

DRAWING PIN

FIG. 6

SHADED PART TO BE CUT AWAY **FIG. 7**

FIG. 8

FIG. 9

SECTIONS AT RIGHT ANGLES WITH SPIRAL

WORK RESTS OVER BENCH VICE

HALF-ROUND FILE

FIG. 10

FIG. 11

FIG. 2. PITCH AND DEPTH OF TWIST. FIG. 3. MARKING THE SQUARE. FIG. 4. CORNERS PLANED OFF. FIG. 5. PRELIMIN-ARY MARKING OF RINGS. FIG. 6. MARKING THE SPIRAL. FIG. 7. WHERE THE GROOVE IS WORKED. FIG. 8. USING V TOOL. FIG. 9. TAKING OFF CORNERS. FIGS. 10 and 11. FINISHING OFF WITH THE HALF-ROUND FILE

Careful Setting Out Ensures A Constant Pitch

HOW THE WORK IS HELD IN THE VICE WHILST BEING CARVED
Note also the double-bine open twist shown to the left of the photograph.

passing down the leg as in Fig. 7, and it is the wood between 1-3 that is to be hollowed out. It is shown shaded in Fig. 7, and it is in fact a good plan to scribble between these lines on the actual leg so that there is no question as to what is to be cut away.

Incidentally, we may note that it is always as well to have a hollow at both ends of the spiral as the latter can then die out naturally. Hence the rings XY at the ends in Fig. 5.

Cutting the Groove.—A carver's V tool is convenient for the preliminary cutting out (see A, Fig. 8) but a carver's gouge can be used throughout if preferred. Gradually deepen the cut until the sides line up with the pencil lines.

Of course, the direction of the cut will have to change during every stroke and it should be in alignment with the spiral the whole time. The best way of holding the work is in the bench vice, cutting away each exposed part of the groove, giving a slight turn, then cutting the newly exposed part, and so on until the whole is completed.

The gouge follows as at B, Fig. 8, care being taken to make the depth as equal as possible throughout. The sides should slope outwards

slightly as at B. At all events avoid undercutting as at C. Once again let the gouge follow the line of the spiral.

Finishing the Rounds.—Using either chisel or flat gouge, take off the corners now as in Fig. 9. You will find that one side will cut easily ; the wood will have to be reversed for the other to be done. Working in this way you will find that the work will approximate roughly to the finished shape.

To take out chisel and gouge marks a large round or a half-round file is used.

If a compound movement is adopted the high parts will automatically be taken out. The flat side of the file can be used for the rounded parts. Rest the work just above the vice as in Fig. 10, so that it can be revolved with the left hand whilst the file is used. Note from Fig. 1 how at the ends the round diminishes into the circular hollow.

Glasspaper is used finally, and it is essential that this is thorough. A shaped rubber can be used, but the fingers are also handy. Follow round the course of the spiral using first *Middle* 2 grade, then finer until you complete with No. 0. In this way you will finish with a beautifully smooth surface.

THE DOUBLE-BINE OPEN TWIST

This open, double-bine twist was used for light table legs during the 17th century. It could be used with admirable effect for a candlestick and can be done entirely without a lathe.

THERE is nothing specially difficult about making the double twist shown in Fig. 5, provided that care is taken in the preliminary setting out and that the work is done in stages. There are, however, one or two snags to be avoided, one of which is that the bines must not be too thin

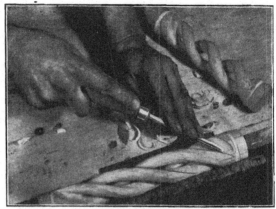

FIG. 1. FINISHING THE ENDS OF THE HOLLOW GROOVES
Here the triple-bine twist is being shaped, but the process is similar. The double-bine can be seen to the right. The whole thing can be made entirely without a lathe.

because this will merely result in a fragile thing which is useless for all practical purposes. It may easily happen as a result of inexperience in cutting even when stouter bines were intended. A second point is that the pitch of the spiral must be at a happy medium. Too low a pitch means that the bines are necessarily thin and are weak owing to there being so much short grain, and a leg made in this way would be useless since it could move in and out like a concertina. On the other hand, an extremely high pitch would not be successful because the twist would be so light as to have an almost accidental appearance.

Setting Out.—It is as well at the outset to understand a little of the principle to be followed when setting out the shape. It is obvious from Fig. 2 that there are two separate and distinct bines, and that each is a replica of the other. It is clear also that the lower the pitch the smaller the bines must be because there is a greater number of twists to get into the same height. Another point is that, although the bines are approximately circular in section when cut through at right angles with their direction (see V, Fig. 2) they are necessarily elliptical when the section is taken across at right angles with the leg itself. This is made clear at AA, Fig. 2.

If you have no lathe you can plane up a piece of square stuff to a circular section. Mark out as shown in Fig. 3. At both ends draw two diameters at right angles with each other, making sure that the two ends line up. This is

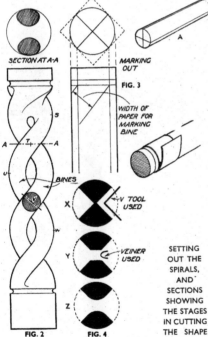

SECTION AT A·A

MARKING OUT

FIG. 3

WIDTH OF PAPER FOR MARKING BINE

FIG. 2

FIG. 4

SETTING OUT THE SPIRALS, AND SECTIONS SHOWING THE STAGES IN CUTTING THE SHAPE

V TOOL USED

VEINER USED

BINES

37

THE SAME IDEA CAN BE CARRIED OUT WITH THREE BINES

easily done if the work is prepared from squares (see dotted lines) since the marks can be gauged in from the flat surfaces. The wood is rounded afterwards, the corners being taken off first to form an octagon. Draw in lines along the length of the wood in line with the diameters drawn at the ends. This is clear from Fig. 3, A. The ends are now divided into four quarters, in two of which the bines will be carved, the remaining two being cut away entirely (see section A-A, Fig. 2).

Now a word about pitch. If you make this somewhere in the region of that shown in Fig. 2, it will not be far out ; a little more or less will not make a lot of difference. However, the pitch must be decided now.

Drawing the Spiral.—Draw in the lines of the small hollow members which occur near the top and bottom, wrapping a piece of paper around the wood as shown in Fig. 3. A pencil run round the edge will draw in a true line. Now take a piece of thin cardboard or thick paper, one edge of which is

perfectly straight and, holding the straight edge level with where the diameter line cuts the hollow member line (X, Fig. 6), wrap the paper round the wood spiralwise, keeping it perfectly flat. Approximate the pitch to that in Fig. 2 as far as possible, and push in a drawing pin at each end.

You can now see the width the bine has to be. Mark in where the adjacent diameter meets the paper (1), and, removing the paper, cut it to this width parallel with the other edge. Replace the paper and run a pencil line along both edges, so completing the marking

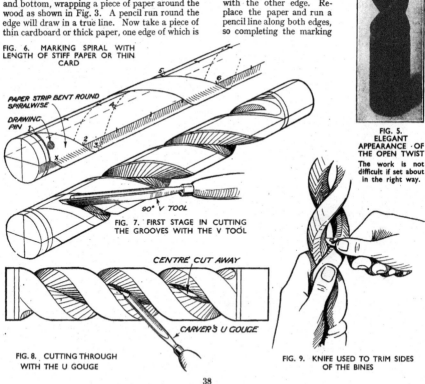

FIG. 6. MARKING SPIRAL WITH LENGTH OF STIFF PAPER OR THIN CARD

PAPER STRIP BENT ROUND SPIRALWISE

DRAWING PIN

90° V TOOL

FIG. 7. FIRST STAGE IN CUTTING THE GROOVES WITH THE V TOOL

CENTRE CUT AWAY

CARVER'S U GOUGE

FIG. 8. CUTTING THROUGH WITH THE U GOUGE

FIG. 5.
ELEGANT APPEARANCE OF THE OPEN TWIST

The work is not difficult if set about in the right way.

FIG. 9. KNIFE USED TO TRIM SIDES OF THE BINES

of one bine. Shift the paper to the next pair of diameter marks and repeat the process, so marking the second bine. If care is taken it will be found that they will be exactly parallel.

Cutting the Spirals.—The V tool is recommended in the opening stages rather than the gouge because with the latter there is the danger that the sides of the bine may be undercut and so reduced in size. The 90 degrees V tool also is preferable because this gives the correct slope automatically. It is shown in use in Fig. 7. Fix the work in the bench vice and starting at about the middle between each bine make a spiral cut. It is, of course, necessary to give the tool a twist as it proceeds along the spiral because it is changing its direction all the time. As it is held in the vice just the top of each section can be cut away. It is then a matter of revolving the wood about one-eighth turn when the cut can be continued. In this way the spiral can be finished from end to end. Do not cut the ends right up to the line because these have to be specially finished.

It will be found that one side of the V tool necessarily cuts more smoothly than the other, the reason, of course, being that it is cutting *with* the grain whilst the other side is working *against* it. The best plan is to cut practically down to the line on the easy cutting side, then reversing the wood in the vice, proceed to finish the other side. Stop the cut about a bare sixteenth inch short of the line. This will produce the effect shown at X in Fig. 4.

Separating the Bines.—You will notice from X, Fig. 4, that this cutting with the V tool leaves only a narrow centre part to be cut away in order to separate the bines. You know from the section in Fig. 2 the finished thickness of the bines and you can now select a carver's gouge (preferably a U-shaped tool) to cut away the remaining wood, so producing the effect shown at Y. The practical work is shown in operation in Fig. 8. Note once again the necessity of altering the direction of the tool so that it cuts steadily along the centre of the groove spiralwise.

Smoothing the Sides.—The best tool to use in the next stage is the ordinary pen-knife with a fairly wide blade sharpened to a super-keen edge. Hold it as shown in Fig. 9 and run round each bine in turn, cutting the edge right up to the line.

The pen-knife will be found more convenient than a carving gouge since it is easier to follow the line of the spiral.

It now remains to finish off each bine to its correct section and the first stage is given at Z, Fig. 4, in which the inner corners are taken off. The waste can be partly removed with either gouge or pen-knife, but it will probably be found more convenient to use a half-round wood file for finishing off. You will find that you can pass this completely between the bines and work it with a compound movement, so taking out all inequalities.

Note that it is always desirable to finish off completely the inner surface of the bines before touching the outer surfaces. The reason for this is that in using the file there is always the danger of the outer surface being damaged, and if the finishing of this is left until last any blemishes can always be taken out. To complete the shape cut away with the gouge or pen-knife the outer corners so that the section shown at AA, Fig. 2, is produced.

The Ends.—The ends need special attention and Fig. 5 should be studied closely. There are various ways in which the finish can be made. At the top the left-hand groove finishes in a small circular cut, that is, it stops short beneath the hollow ring at the top. At the bottom, however, the groove is continued right into the hollow ring.

A rat-tail file will be needed for finishing the crutch between the bines at top and bottom. It is also handy for working into the ends of the groove. For the rest, however, the half-round file is sufficient, using this either flat or round side in accordance with the particular position in which it is working. The file marks can be largely removed by scraping so far as the outer surfaces are concerned, but this is rather more difficult for the inner surfaces, owing to the limited width in which the scraper can work. Some woodworkers keep a special narrow scraper which can be passed between the bines.

In any case, finish off by rubbing thoroughly with glasspaper. Start with a fairly coarse grade, say, middle 2, to take out all inequalities. Follow this with No. 1½, and finally use No. 0. It is really essential to finish off with a very fine grade of glasspaper because it is practically impossible to work the glasspaper in the direction of the grain.

INCISED LETTERING

FIG. I. EXAMPLE OF LETTERING IN PROCESS OF CARVING
This photograph shows some 4 in. letters being cut, and is the work of a reader who has kindly sent it to us. It gives an excellent idea of how effective the result can be.

Although not a difficult task, incised lettering calls for careful cutting if the result is to be successful. The fact is that any irregularity in size or shape is at once noticeable. For a start it is as well to cut fairly large letters, say, 2-4 ins., as the smaller the size the more awkward the work. The incisions are of V-shape and are of an angle of about 70 degrees. The lettering is most effective when cut in oak, and is useful for house name-plates, memorial tablets, etc.

ONE of the most important points to realize at the outset is that nice setting out of the lettering is essential to success. The cleanest cutting in the world looks nothing if the spacing is bad or the shape is poor. The best way is to study any good existing lettering and imitate it. Pick a good Roman alphabet and follow it. The shape will have to be adapted slightly to suit the technique of carving, the serifs* especially being made rather larger and certainly thicker, but the main proportions can be retaining.

Drawing.—Set out the desired wording on a sheet of paper. Draw in parallel lines to give the height, and as a preliminary guide sketch in the letters free hand. A certain amount of trial and error is unavoidable, but once a satisfactory spacing has been secured the whole thing can be put in finally with square and compasses. An adjustable bevel is handy for marking the slope of such letters as A, V, K, etc. When all is in order the whole can be transferred to the wood. One way of doing this is to use carbon paper, but the better plan is to draw in afresh with pencil and square, working exactly from the drawing. It gives a much finer and accurate line to which to work, and by the preliminary drawing in of parallel lines the exact height of all letters is preserved.

This drawing is shown in Fig. 2, and it will be seen

* *Serifs are the ends of the various members of the letters.*

that three lines are put in in every case, the outer ones and that in the centre. The last-named represents, of course, the bottom of the V, and it is necessary for a practical reason that will appear presently. Note that in addition to the centre lines running along the main members of the letters, others are drawn in from the corners of the serifs. They can be drawn in freehand, and they should halve the angle made by the corners. Their purpose is to mark the bottom of the V (you will realize that every part of the incision takes the form of a V). One last point about the drawing. You will see that at the bottom of the P the serif curves upwards slightly in the middle ; the same thing applies where the curve of the P joins the top serif. This adds to the grace of the letter but makes the cutting rather more awkward. It is simpler to mark all such parts straight.

Cutting the Centre.—Now for the actual cutting. A great deal of the work could be done with the V tool only—it is used to a certain extent in any case—but it is a tricky tool to handle successfully unless you have had considerable experience. There is the danger of over-running and of drifting from the line, and the great difficulty of the curves. Altogether the better plan is to remove the wood with sloping cuts, using chisel and gouge. Now to do this cleanly it is essential to make upright cuts first along the centre lines. This enables the wood to be actually *cut* rather than levered away, and it ensures that the bottom of the V is exactly midway between the outer lines.

For the straight parts use a chisel (as wide as possible so that there is less tendency to irregu-

ACCURATE CUTTING IS ESSENTIAL IN LETTERING

larity), and a gouge for the curves, selecting one which approximates as closely as possible to the shape. Cut down vertically. In the case of the upright member the cut is deep, but the ends of the curve are less deep than the rest because, since these parts are narrower, they are automatically shallower. This is made clear at A, Fig. 3. A similar idea applies to such letters as E (Fig. 2), in which the horizontal members are shallow. In the same way the centre cuts of the serifs are deeper at the centre than at the ends, since at the latter the V runs right out (see B, Fig. 3). Incidentally, it is sound policy to cut a sample letter or two in spare wood. You will soon learn the practical advantages of proceeding in a certain way. Fig. 4 shows this preliminary vertical cutting in.

The actual removal of the waste follows, and for the straight parts use a chisel as in Fig. 5. For a start cut a trifle short of the line and work along as far as where the curves spring out. The over-all angle should be about 70 degrees, and it is a good plan to run the V tool along the channel afterwards as this gives the slope. You can finish with this tool if you like, or you can make the final cuts with the chisel. It is all a question of practice. In any case, keep the tools razor sharp, and

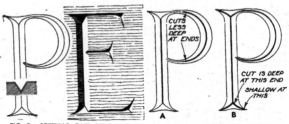

FIG. 2. SETTING OUT OF P AND E
Note the centre lines.

FIG. 3. PRELIMINARY CUTTING
Centre lines are cut in vertically.

try to obtain the effect in as few cuts as possible. A lot of small niggling cuts take longer and are inclined to give a disjointed effect.

For the curves proceed in the same way, but use a gouge which fits the curve. Retain the same angle throughout and remember to taper the cuts towards the ends. You will see that where the lower part of the curve of the P joins the upright member its V extends only a short way down the deep V (Fig. 5).

When cutting the sides of the serifs use the same gouge as that with which you cut in the centre lines, holding it with the hollow side downwards, and taking care to make them flow into the main lines in an unbroken sweep. A flat gouge is handy for the top and bottom, or you can use a knife such as that used in chip carving. Fig. 6 shows the top end in enlarged size.

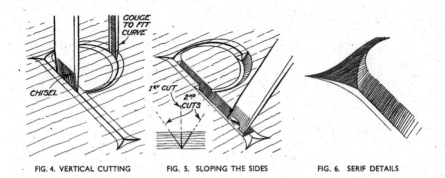

FIG. 4. VERTICAL CUTTING   FIG. 5. SLOPING THE SIDES   FIG. 6. SERIF DETAILS

CHIP CARVING

Although it has scarcely the dignity of carving proper, chip carving is an effective form of decoration, and it combines the advantages of simplicity and of needing few tools. It certainly calls for neatness and dexterity, but once the knack has been acquired it is merely a matter of using patience. The designs, it will be seen, are of an entirely geometrical character, and can be set out easily with square and compass.

FIG. I. SMALL BOX DECORATED WITH SIMPLE CHIP CARVING
In order to give an idea of the scale the above box measures 4½ ins. by 2½ ins. It will be seen that the whole thing consists of a series of V-shaped pockets set out in geometrical form with square and compasses.

YOU will see from an examination of the accompanying illustrations that the carving consists entirely of a series of small pockets or recesses, nearly all of triangular or similar shape. Sometimes they have four or more sides, and occasionally only two, but all are alike in that the sides slope downwards to the centre at an angle. It is thus clear that all the waste can be removed in little flat chips, hence the name by which it is called.

Tools.—The work can be done with either a knife or one or two carving gouges, or both. The writer prefers to use carving gouges as they produce the result more rapidly, especially in hardwood, though a knife is handy on occasion. However, just as good a result can be obtained with a knife.

Special knives for the purpose can be obtained, though they are not essential. For a simple pattern such as that in Fig. 1 only a single knife such as that shown in Fig. 4 is needed. It has an edge at the end as well as at the side, because it is sometimes handier to use the end rather than the side. If carving tools are preferred, the following are handy : ¼ in., No. 4, ⅛ in., No. 4, ¼ in. chisel and ¼ in. skew chisel.

How Pockets are Formed.—We may go straightway to the principle governing all chip carving. At A, Fig. 3, is shown a typical pocket. It consists of three sloping surfaces running in at equal angles from the surface. Where they meet three lines are formed, and, since the slope of the surfaces is the same in every case, the lines always halve the angle from which they spring. This is

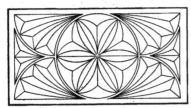

FIG. 2. HOW THE DESIGN IS DRAWN OUT
Note how centre lines are drawn to the pockets in every case.

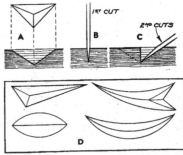

FIG. 3. STAGES IN CUTTING POCKETS (A, B, C)
At D are shown a few typical shapes of pockets.

FIG. 4. TYPE OF KNIFE USED IN CHIP CARVING

ALWAYS KEEP GOUGES & KNIVES RAZOR SHARP

exemplified in the various examples given at D. Precisely the same idea applies in the case of curves. These lines, it will be found, are of considerable importance and need to be set out properly on the design. They are the first to be cut, being set in vertically, reaching deeply in at the lowest part of the pocket and running out at the surface as the ends are reached. This is shown at B, Fig. 3. The following cuts run into these centre ones as at C, the knife or gouge being held at the same angle as the sloping surfaces.

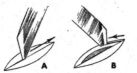

FIG. 5. CUTTING WITH KNIFE
At A the upright centre cut is being made, and at B the sloping cuts which remove the chips.

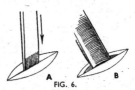

FIG. 6.
USING CHISEL AND GOUGE
The chisel makes the centre cut A, whilst the gouge cuts the waste (B).

Cutting Centre Lines.—It is thus clear that the setting-in of these centre lines serves two purposes. Firstly, it ensures the chips lifting cleanly away since they are actually cut, not merely splintered or scraped out. Secondly, it ensures accuracy, both surfaces meeting upon the centre lines and thus being perforce of the same angle.

Drawing Design.—It follows that when the design is drawn out it is necessary to put in these centre lines (which represent the depressions) as well as the surface lines, which are, of course, the high parts. Fig. 2 shows the drawing required for the small box shown in Fig. 1. The square and compasses are used for the greater part. In the case of the curved fan-like shapes, since these are not circular, the best plan is to step out the width into six equal parts and sketch in the curves free-hand. It is simpler to put in the centre one first and space the others equally at each side. Generally it is best to draw in the design in pencil directly on the wood after a preliminary sketch on paper. It is not advisable to trace the design with carbon paper because in a geometrical design the slightest

inaccuracy shows up badly. The free-hand curves could be traced, but circular curves and straight lines are best drawn directly on the wood to be carved.

Cutting Pockets.—Fig. 5, A, shows the preliminary cut for one of the centre pockets when the knife is used. Beginning lightly at one end, the pressure is increased as the middle is reached, and reduced again towards the other end. Several cuts will probably be needed to reach to the full depth, though this depends upon the hardness of the wood being cut. In the second cut the knife is held over at an angle and the chips cut away as at B. Needless to say, the whole success of the work depends upon keeping carefully to the line and in making clean cuts. The fewer the cuts in which you can complete the job the better the effect. The direction in which the knife is used has to be watched because of the grain. In some cases it may have to be changed in a single cut.

The procedure is similar when gouges are used, but the preliminary centre vertical cut is made by stabbing down with the chisel as at A, Fig. 6. Cutting in with a flat gouge follows as at B. For some of the pockets it would be necessary to use a flat gouge the reverse way round, that is hollow side downwards.

Ten minutes' experimental cutting will teach more than this article can hope to do once the principle of cutting has been grasped.

PANEL WITH SPRAYS OF OAK AND LAUREL
(*Continued from page 33*)

Follow by separating the leaves, berries, etc., and give the local undulations on the individual leaves. Where the stalks rise high above the groundwork, considerable undercutting will be needed in order to give the feeling of roundness. Undercutting is also necessary at the leaf edges, especially where they stand well away from the groundwork. Finally, the groundwork can be

reduced to the finished depth, a broad flat gouge being used. Make any final adjustments to the leaf edges whilst doing so. Incidentally, for such rounded parts as the berries and acorns a gouge can be used with the hollow side downwards. It is used with a rocking movement so that the tool follows round the shape, so giving a nice smooth surface.

FIG. I. PHOTOGRAPH OF THE EGG AND TONGUE MOULDING, PARTLY COMPLETED AND PARTLY IN EARLY STAGE
This is the ideal decoration for a cornice in which a bold effect is required. Regularity in the setting out is essential.

EGG & TONGUE and ACANTHUS LEAF MOULDINGS

Both of these enrichments were widely used during the Renaissance period of furniture. These are, of course, a classical motif and form a most effective means of decorating a moulding. The egg and tongue detail is carved on the ovolo section, and the acanthus leafage on a cyma recta section.

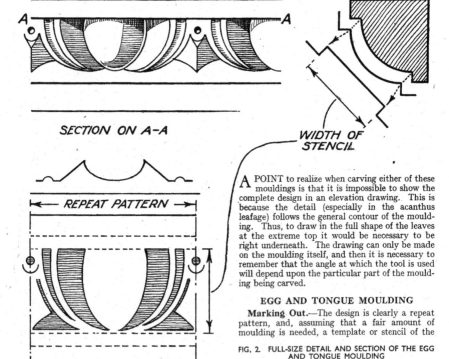

SECTION ON A-A

WIDTH OF STENCIL

REPEAT PATTERN

A POINT to realize when carving either of these mouldings is that it is impossible to show the complete design in an elevation drawing. This is because the detail (especially in the acanthus leafage) follows the general contour of the moulding. Thus, to draw in the full shape of the leaves at the extreme top it would be necessary to be right underneath. The drawing can only be made on the moulding itself, and then it is necessary to remember that the angle at which the tool is used will depend upon the particular part of the moulding being carved.

EGG AND TONGUE MOULDING

Marking Out.—The design is clearly a repeat pattern, and, assuming that a fair amount of moulding is needed, a template or stencil of the

FIG. 2. FULL-SIZE DETAIL AND SECTION OF THE EGG AND TONGUE MOULDING

FIG. 3. EARLY AND ADVANCED STAGES OF THE ACANTHUS LEAF MOULDING. DELICATE CARVING IS NEEDED

design makes a quick way of marking. A drawing is needed for it, and this in a measure is dependent upon whether an exact number of " eggs " is needed to fill a required length. For instance, if the moulding is to be mitred around a cabinet, it would be desirable for the detail to balance at both ends, and it would not do for the mitres to occur at, say, quarter-way through an egg. A certain amount of latitude is generally possible by leaving the ends to be cut finally after the mitres are cut and arranging a special pattern (say, an acanthus leaf) to cover the detail, especially when the joining lengths of moulding make it awkward to arrange a matched or balanced effect. However, it is a point to be thought of when planning out the drawing.

A section of the moulding is given in Fig. 2. Cut a piece of stout paper such as cartridge paper wide enough to wrap over the whole moulding and long enough to include a complete repeat of the pattern. Fold the paper well into the shape of the moulding, creasing the paper where the corners and angles occur. Sketch in the pattern approximately as in Fig. 2 until you have a nice shape, and then draw it in carefully, arranging the length of the repeat in accordance with practical requirements.

To make the stencil you cannot cut all the lines or the pattern would drop to pieces, but you can cut the parts shown shaded in Fig. 2. A coat of french polish at each side will prevent the paper from be-

coming worn and soaking up the stencilling liquid. Use a fairly thick medium for stencilling, such as oil paint, using the minimum quantity and dabbing it on with a stencil brush. Do not use ordinary wood stain as it is liable to creep along the grain and give faulty marking. Clearly, the pattern must link up exactly when the repeat is marked. The surest way is to measure the repeat pattern along the moulding, stepping with dividers, and making the stencil line up with the marks.

Cutting In.—The wood at each side of the eggs should be cut away first, and it is clearly necessary to preserve both inner and outer lines as only in this way can the shape of the egg and chamfer be preserved when the full depth is reached. A certain amount of waste can be removed with a U tool or small, quick gouge, but take care to keep it inside the stencil mark edge, and do not cut in too deeply

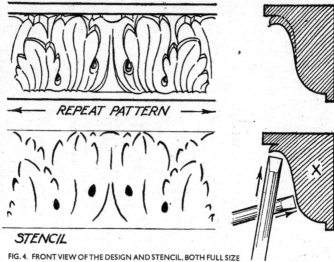

REPEAT PATTERN

STENCIL

FIG. 4. FRONT VIEW OF THE DESIGN AND STENCIL, BOTH FULL SIZE

45

or the chamfer surface may be spoilt. The advantage of the U tool is that it eases the final cutting.

Now hold a gouge on the line of the egg and chop straight down, choosing a gouge to suit the curve. Slope away the wood up to the chamfer line, using a flat gouge. The effect of this is shown to the left in Fig. 1. The depth of the cut is purely a matter of judgment. When a long length of moulding has to be carved a good plan is to cut one complete egg on a spare piece of moulding, and move this along as the work proceeds as a guide to keeping the whole the same depth. To make the eggs smooth a gouge should be used hollow side downwards. Use a gouge *slightly* flatter than the curve to prevent digging in at the corners, and change the tool to suit the particular part of the egg being carved. This is one of the occasions in carving in which tool marks should be eliminated as far as possible.

Detail.—The little dots can be cut with a very small gouge, revolving the latter between the hands ; a punch can be used to finish off. The quick cut beneath the dot is cut in ; also the curves which slope from it. Ease away the wood from each side. Afterwards the point of the tongue is formed by downward cuts, the waste wood being pared away flat with the quirk of the moulding. Finally, the little tapering hollows are run in along the straps.

ACANTHUS LEAF MOULDING

The effect of this is more delicate than the more robust egg and tongue. One of the great masters of its application was Wren who made wonderful use of it in his cornices. In a general way the marking out is similar. The stiff paper is wrapped around the moulding and the corners and angles sketched in.

Note that there is a main centre leaf with two smaller subsidiary leaves at each side, each overlapping its neighbour. . Each complete leaf is subdivided into separate lobes, each of which comes within an imaginary outline. Draw in the veins and other high parts which form the general contour.

Fig. 4 shows how a stencil can be prepared. Note how ties are left at intervals to hold the whole thing together. If preferred, the design could be simplified—in fact, for a moulding smaller than that given, it would be essential. In any case this leafwork is difficult to do cleanly, and should certainly not be the subject of an early effort in wood carving. Cut in a complete repeat in the stencil and mark out on the wood, being careful to make the marks coincide.

Setting In.—A certain limited amount of modelling can be carried out, but this cannot be done at an early stage because it would mean that the marks on the wood were cut away. The first essential is to separate the main leaves from each other where they overlap, and this is done as shown to the left and right in Fig. 3. A cut is made around the general outline of the leaves, the individual lobes being ignored at this stage. On the waste side the wood is sloped into the cuts. As in every case the general lines flow from eyes where the leaves fold one over the other, the eyes can be cut in first. They should be deep because the leaf is supposed to be pierced right through. Use a very small gouge and then punch in deeply. The latter saves an awkward cleaning-out operation. Where the leaves strike the top edge of the moulding much of the waste can be cut away (Fig. 3).

Now follows the general modelling. Watch carefully the general line of the veins, keeping them flowing and symmetrical. The tool must be extremely keen, and the contour of the moulding must be retained. This means carefully raising or lowering the handle as the tool passes across the moulding. Finally, the individual lobes can be set in and cut. Of course, the final modelling cannot be completed until this detail has been set in.

OAK TRAY WITH CARVED CORNERS. *See page 25.*

46